Complete Hor

Sagittarius 2022

Monthly astrological forecasts for 2022

TATIANA BORSCH

Contents

2022 – A World Still in Flux

We survived the incredible stress of 2020-2021, when our world's very foundation seemed to be falling apart under us. What does 2022 have in store?

According to the stars, the coming year can be divided into two distinct periods: a very favorable time during the first half of the year, and trouble during the second half.

Politics and Economy

From January to July, things will be serene and predictable.

Jupiter and Neptune will dominate this period, and nearly all year long, they will have very strong energy in Pisces. Jupiter's contact with other planets, including Uranus and Pluto, will be exceptionally favorable during the first half of 2022, so we can count on calm, steady waters...

Together in Pisces, Jupiter and Neptune rule the areas of medicine, oil, space, and the sea. Their favorable aspects mean that this is where we can expect a lot of developments in 2022. In addition to medicine, oil, and space, Jupiter and Neptune also rule the arts, so we can expect incredible feats in film, music, and painting. Many of these pieces will have a space or maritime theme.

Neptune also rules everything related to drugs and alcohol, and 2022 may bring a trend toward legalizing drugs in many countries. This will mainly include "soft" drugs, such as marijuana. This is also a promising time for the wine industry, and Jupiter's powerful influence means that we might see increasing production, and more public attention on elite, luxury wine brands.

For now, we will still have to deal with problems related to the economy, but during the first half of the year, they will likely be somewhat mitigated and under control. One way or another the world will start to shake off the coronavirus epidemic, with help from vaccines and new, effective treatments.

Many countries, including Russia, the United States, and China, will rebuild their economies, and shift their direction and approach. Here, we can consider China as the unrefuted global leader.

During the first half of the year, we might see cryptocurrencies experience serious growth, along with the emergence of new cryptocurrencies.

Things are looking less sunny for the EU countries. Despite the fact that the interminable lockdowns will finally come to an end, economies will continue to struggle, and political clashes will continue.

However, during the first half of the year, from January until mid-August, these negative trends will be somewhat less noticeable.

Things in the United States are looking much more peaceful, though Republicans will become more powerful and influential in 2022.

During the first half of the year, the political horizon of our turbulent world is looking relatively quiet. There will be a trend toward resalable relationships toward war and peace, and there may even be major agreements between countries, which will be largely responsible for this state of affairs.

Beginning in the second half of August 2022, however, things will suddenly take a dark turn. Confrontation from Mars is the theme of the second half of the year. This will lead to negativity, crises, and war. In May 2022, Jupiter will also shift from neutral Pisces to belligerent Aries.

The international stage will once again become difficult, and many countries will fail to shoulder their agreements, with hotspots popping up all over the globe. This may become extremely challenging, as Uranus, an abrupt planet full of the unexpected, will be in the same degree of Taurus that it was in 1938, which was a fateful year for the entire world.

Remember that 1938 was the year that Germany, Poland, and Romania divided Czechoslovakia with the agreement of England and France. From an astrological point of view, this is the event that triggered World War Two. Of course, astrology is not alone here – when describing the dissolution of Czechoslovakia, Winston Churchill himself stated that "England has been offered a choice between war and shame. She has chosen shame, and will get war."

Uranus has an 84-year cycle. Its passage through Taurus has always brought large-scale war, including in 1853-1856, with the Crimean Wars, between the Russian Empire and a coalition made up of Britain, France, the Ottoman Empire, and Sardinia.

Uranus entered Taurus on May 5, 2018, and will remain there until April 26, 2026. We already know that between 2018 and 2021, military tensions have escalated around the world. Unfortunately, this is only the beginning of what may continue for a long time into the future.

Warmongering rhetoric and possibly even clashes in hotspots will be more common during the second half of the year, but this will result in the weakening of NATO countries, with China and Russia growing stronger. This may continue into 2023-2024.

During this time, many countries will experience spontaneous protests and unrest. People will begin to resist authority much more strongly, which will force authorities to make some concessions and adopt certain measures, as many countries will find themselves moving closer to revolution. Countries suffering from economic instability are likely to see changes in government, if not outright political chaos.

The horoscope for the United States indicates that in the second half of 2022, there will be turbulence as well as the revelation of certain secrets. Former President Donald Trump will take on an active role and should not be written off. His influence on US citizens will only grow, but political positions will in general become more hardline. All of that will go along with a serious struggle and clashes with democratic institutions.

Protests and unrest are to be expected in Russia, too, during this time. However, President Putin will hold onto power, though there may be some changes to various government bodies. The changes that began with changes in government in 2020 may continue. Of course, some people will suffer, but overall, this will be a good thing for society.

The economic and political situation in Ukraine may worsen in the long term. Military activity in the eastern territories of Luhansk and Donetsk will continue, and that may end poorly for Kyiv, and it will become clear that these territories will never be returned to Ukraine.

Problems that arise during the second half of 2022 will continue during the three months of 2023.

Climate

The climate will continue to change. Jupiter and Neptune will bring major floods that are worse than what we have seen in the last several years. People living in coastal areas should consider this and take the utmost precautions when preparing for spring. Volcanos will also become more active. Glaciers will continue melting, and there is nothing we can do to halt this process.

In late May, Jupiter will move into fiery Aries, and remain there until the end of October. This means that during this time, we can expect fires to break out around the world, causing major ecological and human losses.

In seismically active zones, we can expect major earthquakes.

Health

In 2022, we may see new, unique treatments for serious illnesses such as diabetes and cancer.

From May to November, people should be very careful if they suffer from heart disease or various allergies. In the fall and winter of 2022, we might see new outbreaks of respiratory infections.

During the second half of 2022, we might also see the emergence of new types of diseases. We may also learn new information about the manmade origins of coronavirus, which dominated our world in 2020 and 2021.

Personal Life

The first half of 2022 is a good time for buying real estate or opening up a business.

Single people might meet someone special, and Pisces, those born in the first ten days of Aries, as well as Virgo and Capricorn will be ahead of the rest of the planet in this regard.

Any marriages that take place between January and May are sure to be stable and happy.

Children born in 2022 might grow up to be talented musicians, highly creative, and have extrasensory abilities. In time, they will become inspiring leaders who will steer the world to a positive place.

During the fall and winter of 2022, things will be rocker in politics as well as personal relations. Many people will reconsider their links to others, and a real crisis or breakdown is likely.

If that is your case, remember that any crisis and break with the past is the key to true change, new opportunities, and a new life! This is the only way we can deal with the twists and turns Fate throws our way!

2022 Overview for Sagittarius

2022 may tear you to pieces – at work, at home, in your relationships... But remember – things might look daunting, but whenever you get to work, things start to look up. With this in mind, you will be able to get back on the horse and in fighting form in no time.

Work. During the first half of the year, entrepreneurs and managers at every level will be thinking about expanding their business. You might acquire real estate, land, or start major construction. If you already began that in 2021, you will continue those efforts in 2022.

During the first half of the year, you can expect smooth sailing at work – slowly, but surely, you are working toward your goals and by late summer, you will reap the results.

You might reconnect with former business partners and old friends who now live in another city or abroad.

However, in October, things will suddenly take a sharp turn – aggressive Mars will begin conflict with your ruler, Jupiter. This portends a difficult streak. Specifically, someone will try to take away your property, or something you consider yours. Your opponents may look differently – perhaps they are an auditing agency, or enemies and competitors who may be working against you covertly or in the open.

In sum, get ready to defend yourself and begin gathering allies in advance. Go even further and assemble a team you can count on when the going gets tough. The stars are suspicious of your current assistants – most of them may not be competent or reliable.

Employees can expect trouble on their teams – there may be changes underway at work, changes in leadership, or other types of events that led to the Chinese expression "God forbid you live through changes". Keep your head down and do not go to your managers with any needs – they will neither listen you nor provide any help.

This time of troubles will last until late December or 2023, when people will say "Don't judge the winners!" when they talk about you.

Money. Financially speaking, the first half of the year will be positive. You may have your own salary in addition to favorable terms of credit, profit from successful real estate transactions, and even an inheritance. You may count on help from your parents or loved ones.

From October to December, things will be less sunny – though you will be able to ensure that everything you earned previously does not go up in smoke.

Love and family. If you are more focused on your personal life, the stars predict a series of changes headed your way. Couples who get along might buy a new home, apartment, or summer home, and the first half of the year is a great time for this. However, be sure to look over any documents carefully when undertaking such a major, fateful task. During the second half of the year, you can expect situations that will shed doubt on the reliability of what you have built or purchased.

Couples whose relationship is on the rocks might begin divorce proceedings, and will clash over their apartment, home, summer home, or other property. Your partner will take a rigid stance, and be unyielding, aggressive, and in the worst cases, he or she will drag you into court. You will not be able to reach a compromise until late December, and your children may act as peacemakers.

You will feel Jupiter's influence on your personal life during the summer. Single people will easily find romance, but are unlikely to be ready for things to last very long. You may face a conflict of interest, demands from a new lover, or possibly, things will flame out and there will be nothing left to salvage.

Alternatively, you will be torn between an old relationship and someone new, and that is never an easy predicament to be in. Any unfaithful spouses or those trying to decide between two people should keep in mind that this fall, all of your skeletons will be dragged out of the closet.

The eclipses of 2022 will shed light on a lot of secrets. Don't forget that if you are keeping things from your partner, no matter your field or marital status.

Health. In 2022, you are feeling sluggish, so do not push your own limits and practice moderation. Many Sagittarians might tend to gain weight in 2022, so do not forget to exercise, spend time in nature, and naturally, follow a balanced diet.

January

New York Time			London Time		
Calendar Day	Lunar Day	Lunar Day Start Time	Calendar Day	Lunar Day	Lunar Day Start Time
01/01/2022	29	6:06 AM	01/01/2022	29	6:42 AM
02/01/2022	30	7:10 AM	02/01/2022	30	7:49 AM
02/01/2022	1	1:35 PM	02/01/2022	1	6:35 PM
03/01/2022	2	8:06 AM	03/01/2022	2	8:42 AM
04/01/2022	3	8:51 AM	04/01/2022	3	9:21 AM
05/01/2022	4	9:29 AM	05/01/2022	4	9:51 AM
06/01/2022	5	10:01 AM	06/01/2022	5	10:15 AM
07/01/2022	6	10:30 AM	07/01/2022	6	10:36 AM
08/01/2022	7	10:56 AM	08/01/2022	7	10:54 AM
09/01/2022	8	11:23 AM	09/01/2022	8	11:12 AM
10/01/2022	9	11:49 AM	10/01/2022	9	11:30 AM
11/01/2022	10	12:18 PM	11/01/2022	10	11:51 AM
12/01/2022	11	12:50 PM	12/01/2022	11	12:15 PM
13/01/2022	12	1:27 PM	13/01/2022	12	12:44 PM
14/01/2022	13	2:08 PM	14/01/2022	13	1:20 PM
15/01/2022	14	2:56 PM	15/01/2022	14	2:05 PM
16/01/2022	15	3:49 PM	16/01/2022	15	2:58 PM
17/01/2022	16	4:46 PM	17/01/2022	16	3:58 PM
18/01/2022	17	5:47 PM	18/01/2022	17	5:05 PM
19/01/2022	18	6:49 PM	19/01/2022	18	6:15 PM
20/01/2022	19	7:52 PM	20/01/2022	19	7:26 PM
21/01/2022	20	8:56 PM	21/01/2022	20	8:38 PM
22/01/2022	21	10:00 PM	22/01/2022	21	9:52 PM
23/01/2022	22	11:06 PM	23/01/2022	22	11:06 PM
25/01/2022	23	12:14 AM	25/01/2022	23	12:23 AM
26/01/2022	24	1:24 AM	26/01/2022	24	1:42 AM
27/01/2022	25	2:35 AM	27/01/2022	25	3:02 AM
28/01/2022	26	3:45 AM	28/01/2022	26	4:19 AM
29/01/2022	27	4:51 AM	29/01/2022	27	5:30 AM
30/01/2022	28	5:50 AM	30/01/2022	28	6:28 AM
31/01/2022	29	6:40 AM	31/01/2022	29	7:13 AM

You can find the description of each lunar day in the chapter "A Guide to The Moon Cycle and Lunar Days"

The first month of 2022 will be an auspicious time for you. But if you haven't made your first million yet, there's never been a better time to start!

Work. It's hard for you to relax as you settle into January. First of all, you will have to deal with a variety of administrative issues, as the work doesn't wait.

Many Sagittarians are dealing with concerns related to real estate. Entrepreneurs are thinking of expanding their business, and have their eye on new facilities with this in mind. These concerns may be in the background all year long.

Things are going well for those who are employees, too. If you got a recent job offer, now, you are thinking about how to strengthen your position.

Those who are not satisfied with their current jobs may be thinking about opening their own business, and taking some steps in that direction.

Your relationship with colleagues in other cities or abroad is moving along and you are seeing success, which will be most noticeable during the second half of the month. There is nothing new here, you have seen these issues before, and now you know how to respond. To be fair, these challenges will gradually resolve themselves, so remember, "He who tries wins" has never been more appropriate.

Money. Your finances are really looking up this month. Money will be coming in regularly, and there will be noticeably more of it, too. Expect to receive the largest sums on January 2, 3, 11, 12, 21, 22, 29, and 30. Expect it to come from both official and unofficial sources.

Love and family. A lot of decisive events are taking place in your personal life. Many will make drastic changes in their day-to-day lives, whether that means moving to a new apartment, building a home, cottage, or something else – maybe you will start major repairs on your current home.

During the second half of the month, your relationship with a relative will become difficult, most likely due to old arguments and unresolved issues from the past.

Couples will not be particularly happy in January, but they also will not suffer. If your relationship is smooth and stable, it will remain that way. If that is not the case, things might get worse. In either case, keep an eye on your loved ones and hold your tongue – your criticism might have the opposite of the intended effect in January.

Single people should keep in mind that anyone new you meet in January is unlikely to be reliable. They may disappear, leaving behind nothing but unpleasant memories.

Health. You are feeling a bit sluggish this month, so take care of yourself and remember that moderation is the key. Be careful on any trips or while driving – this is especially the case during the second half of the month.

The stars suggest avoiding any travel to faraway places, unless you absolutely have to. If you do travel anyway, choose a place you have been to before.

February

New York Time			London Time		
Calendar Day	Lunar Day	Lunar Day Start Time	Calendar Day	Lunar Day	Lunar Day Start Time
01/02/2022	1	12:49 AM	01/02/2022	1	5:49 AM
01/02/2022	2	7:22 AM	01/02/2022	2	7:48 AM
02/02/2022	3	7:57 AM	02/02/2022	3	8:15 AM
03/02/2022	4	8:28 AM	03/02/2022	4	8:38 AM
04/02/2022	5	8:56 AM	04/02/2022	5	8:57 AM
05/02/2022	6	9:23 AM	05/02/2022	6	9:16 AM
06/02/2022	7	9:50 AM	06/02/2022	7	9:35 AM
07/02/2022	8	10:19 AM	07/02/2022	8	9:55 AM
08/02/2022	9	10:50 AM	08/02/2022	9	10:18 AM
09/02/2022	10	11:25 AM	09/02/2022	10	10:45 AM
10/02/2022	11	12:04 PM	10/02/2022	11	11:18 AM
11/02/2022	12	12:50 PM	11/02/2022	12	11:59 AM
12/02/2022	13	1:40 PM	12/02/2022	13	12:49 PM
13/02/2022	14	2:36 PM	13/02/2022	14	1:47 PM
14/02/2022	15	3:36 PM	14/02/2022	15	2:52 PM
15/02/2022	16	4:38 PM	15/02/2022	16	4:01 PM
16/02/2022	17	5:42 PM	16/02/2022	17	5:13 PM
17/02/2022	18	6:47 PM	17/02/2022	18	6:26 PM
18/02/2022	19	7:52 PM	18/02/2022	19	7:40 PM
19/02/2022	20	8:58 PM	19/02/2022	20	8:56 PM
20/02/2022	21	10:06 PM	20/02/2022	21	10:12 PM
21/02/2022	22	11:15 PM	21/02/2022	22	11:31 PM
23/02/2022	23	12:25 AM	23/02/2022	23	12:50 AM
24/02/2022	24	1:34 AM	24/02/2022	24	2:07 AM
25/02/2022	25	2:40 AM	25/02/2022	25	3:18 AM
26/02/2022	26	3:40 AM	26/02/2022	26	4:19 AM
27/02/2022	27	4:31 AM	27/02/2022	27	5:08 AM
28/02/2022	28	5:15 AM	28/02/2022	28	5:45 AM

You can find the description of each lunar day in the chapter "A Guide to The Moon Cycle and Lunar Days"

In February, you will be incredibly active. So much that you will even surprise those close to you, who are already aware that you are a ball of energy with a nonstop stream of ideas. Luck is on your side, so buckle up!

Work. Everything is coming up roses for you at work and when it comes to anything professional this month. Entrepreneurs and managers can count on some new and beneficial deals, as well as some additional profits from work you completed earlier.

Employees can expect new job offers that might be a big step up from your current position. The ball is in your court, and that's always a good thing!

Your relationship with colleagues in other cities or abroad is moving along nicely, though some problems from prior months are no longer so pressing, and any remaining issues can be dealt with later.

Any transactions involving real estate that you began in the recent past are moving forward in your favor.

Money. This month is one of the best of the year for your bank account. Money will be coming in regularly, and there will be noticeably more of it. In addition to your usual earnings, you can count on profits from unofficial sources.

Employees might get a bonus or money from a second job. Expect the largest amounts on February 4, 7, 8, 17, 18, 22, 26, and 27.

Love and family. Some big changes are on the horizon when it comes to your personal life. You may begin or continue major repairs or construction. There is also a possibility of obtaining a new apartment, home, or summer home, maybe in another city or abroad.

Your family is getting along, and partners with a friendly relationship are tackling some challenging domestic issues, and this month there will be a lot of them. Your relationship with some relatives has suffered in the recent past. Things will remain as they are, as they say, "no peace, no war".

It is hard to say what is in store for those in a romantic relationship, as February is so focused on work and your home itself. The exception is those who are, as fate has it, tied to someone born under the sign of Capricorn. If that is your case, expect your relationship to develop very rapidly, which will be rather useful at work, too.

Health. You are feeling full of energy in February and unlikely to experience any illness.

March

New York Time			London Time		
Calendar Day	Lunar Day	Lunar Day Start Time	Calendar Day	Lunar Day	Lunar Day Start Time
01/03/2022	29	5:53 AM	01/03/2022	29	6:15 AM
02/03/2022	30	6:25 AM	02/03/2022	30	6:39 AM
02/03/2022	1	12:38 PM	02/03/2022	1	5:38 PM
03/03/2022	2	6:54 AM	03/03/2022	2	7:00 AM
04/03/2022	3	7:22 AM	04/03/2022	3	7:19 AM
05/03/2022	4	7:49 AM	05/03/2022	4	7:38 AM
06/03/2022	5	8:18 AM	06/03/2022	5	7:57 AM
07/03/2022	6	8:48 AM	07/03/2022	6	8:19 AM
08/03/2022	7	9:22 AM	08/03/2022	7	8:45 AM
09/03/2022	8	10:00 AM	09/03/2022	8	9:16 AM
10/03/2022	9	10:43 AM	10/03/2022	9	9:54 AM
11/03/2022	10	11:31 AM	11/03/2022	10	10:40 AM
12/03/2022	11	12:25 PM	12/03/2022	11	11:34 AM
13/03/2022	12	1:23 PM	13/03/2022	12	12:36 PM
14/03/2022	13	2:24 PM	14/03/2022	13	1:44 PM
15/03/2022	14	3:27 PM	15/03/2022	14	2:55 PM
16/03/2022	15	4:32 PM	16/03/2022	15	4:08 PM
17/03/2022	16	5:38 PM	17/03/2022	16	5:23 PM
18/03/2022	17	6:45 PM	18/03/2022	17	6:39 PM
19/03/2022	18	7:54 PM	19/03/2022	18	7:57 PM
20/03/2022	19	9:05 PM	20/03/2022	19	9:17 PM
21/03/2022	20	10:16 PM	21/03/2022	20	10:37 PM
22/03/2022	21	11:26 PM	22/03/2022	21	11:57 PM
24/03/2022	22	12:34 AM	24/03/2022	22	1:10 AM
25/03/2022	23	1:35 AM	25/03/2022	23	2:14 AM
26/03/2022	24	2:28 AM	26/03/2022	24	3:06 AM
27/03/2022	25	3:13 AM	27/03/2022	25	4:46 AM
28/03/2022	26	3:52 AM	28/03/2022	26	5:17 AM
29/03/2022	27	4:25 AM	29/03/2022	27	5:42 AM
30/03/2022	28	4:54 AM	30/03/2022	28	6:04 AM
31/03/2022	29	5:22 AM	31/03/2022	29	6:23 AM

You can find the description of each lunar day in the chapter "A Guide to The Moon Cycle and Lunar Days"

It's time to forget about work, let your hair down, and relax a little. If you really feel like working, focus your efforts on your home and family affairs. All of that is important, right now.

Work. If you are one of those incorrigible workaholics who just can't switch it off, March is a time for you to get all your papers in order, organize your office, or maybe even work on expanding your business. That is the most likely scenario for any entrepreneurs or managers who are feeling restless these days. You may be acquiring new real estate or busy with major repairs.

The challenge this month might be in your relationship with colleagues from other cities or abroad. You might see unexpected difficulties, changes to existing agreements, or simply circumstances over which you have no control.

You might see some roadblocks with planned trips or misunderstandings along the way. If you have plans to go on a business trip, examine every possible outcome to make sure you don't end up stuck somewhere. You may face various limitations similar to what we experienced during the pandemic.

Money. Your financial situation is stable and is showing a significant upward trend. In addition to your usual salary, this month you can also count on additional income. That may stem from real estate transactions or some favorable credit. You may also get help from your parents, a loved one, or a spouse.

Love and family. Many people this month are fully immersed in their personal lives. Anyone planning any renovations might experience a real breakthrough in such a difficult, cumbersome task. You might even be busy building a new home, acquiring an apartment, summer home, or land. In some cases, you may simply be making plans related to your home, and in others, you may actually be right in the thick of it.

Many families will have to grapple with challenges involving your relationship with relatives. Old problems may rear their ugly heads again, and you will have to put some elbow grease into solving them.

In March, many will feel the desire to get away from it all for a little, and you will find time for it. But if you are planning a trip, keep in mind it may not actually happen for reasons beyond your control.

Health. This month, you are feeling healthy, but the stars recommend you take extra care when driving and be more careful while traveling.

In March, many Sagittarians will tend to put on some weight, so the stars recommend avoiding any excess calories and follow some folk wisdom here – "breakfast like a king, lunch like a queen, and dinner like a pauper."

April

New York Time				London Time		
Calendar Day	Lunar Day	Lunar Day Start Time		Calendar Day	Lunar Day	Lunar Day Start Time
01/04/2022	1	1:27 AM		01/04/2022	30	6:41 AM
01/04/2022	2	5:49 AM		01/04/2022	1	7:27 AM
02/04/2022	3	6:17 AM		02/04/2022	2	7:00 AM
03/04/2022	4	6:47 AM		03/04/2022	3	7:21 AM
04/04/2022	5	7:19 AM		04/04/2022	4	7:45 AM
05/04/2022	6	7:55 AM		05/04/2022	5	8:14 AM
06/04/2022	7	8:37 AM		06/04/2022	6	8:49 AM
07/04/2022	8	9:23 AM		07/04/2022	7	9:32 AM
08/04/2022	9	10:14 AM		08/04/2022	8	10:23 AM
09/04/2022	10	11:10 AM		09/04/2022	9	11:22 AM
10/04/2022	11	12:09 PM		10/04/2022	10	12:26 PM
11/04/2022	12	1:11 PM		11/04/2022	11	1:35 PM
12/04/2022	13	2:14 PM		12/04/2022	12	2:46 PM
13/04/2022	14	3:19 PM		13/04/2022	13	4:00 PM
14/04/2022	15	4:26 PM		14/04/2022	14	5:15 PM
15/04/2022	16	5:35 PM		15/04/2022	15	6:33 PM
16/04/2022	17	6:46 PM		16/04/2022	16	7:54 PM
17/04/2022	18	7:59 PM		17/04/2022	17	9:16 PM
18/04/2022	19	9:12 PM		18/04/2022	18	10:39 PM
19/04/2022	20	10:23 PM		19/04/2022	19	11:58 PM
20/04/2022	21	11:29 PM		21/04/2022	20	1:07 AM
22/04/2022	22	12:25 AM		22/04/2022	21	2:04 AM
23/04/2022	23	1:13 AM		23/04/2022	22	2:48 AM
24/04/2022	24	1:53 AM		24/04/2022	23	3:21 AM
25/04/2022	25	2:28 AM		25/04/2022	24	3:48 AM
26/04/2022	26	2:58 AM		26/04/2022	25	4:10 AM
27/04/2022	27	3:25 AM		27/04/2022	26	4:29 AM
28/04/2022	28	3:52 AM		28/04/2022	27	4:47 AM
29/04/2022	29	4:19 AM		29/04/2022	28	5:05 AM
30/04/2022	30	4:47 AM		30/04/2022	29	5:25 AM
30/04/2022	1	4:30 PM		30/04/2022	1	9:30 PM

You can find the description of each lunar day in the chapter "A Guide to The Moon Cycle and Lunar Days"

Throughout April, your trump card is your incredible reaction and ability to make out-of-the-box decisions. These skills have always been up your sleeve, and now they're finally getting noticed!

Work. For anything work-related, this month is looking up. Both managers and entrepreneurs can count on new, beneficial offers for everyone, along with a good outlook for the future. Your relationship with your team has significantly improved, whether you are an entrepreneur or employee. Any issues in the recent past are looking very different in April – they are less acute and closer to resolution. You might also get some new colleagues who will turn out to be hardworking, professional, and responsible.

Those who are dealing with a series of thorny issues involving partners from other cities or abroad are able to resolve them, at least in part. Given the difficult past and less-than-stable future, that is a very good thing. In short, April is a good time that you should take full advantage of.

Money. This month, your finances are looking great. You might profit handsomely from recent work and the future is looking hopeful, too.

Those who are busy with various types of real estate transactions might also count on some nice profits. This might include acquiring property on favorable terms or a successful sale. Even troublesome and expensive repairs will go smoothly this month, and be less of a financial burden than you think.

Love and family. Your personal life is also interesting this month. As in the past, your main task with your family might be acquiring a new home, construction, or major repairs. This time, however, you can expect some big changes, and in some cases, completing the major steps.

In a lucky coincidence, your finances are currently sufficient to provide support for a loved one – this will allow you to do a good deed and bring yourself closer to your aims.

Your relationship with your children is much warmer, and this month you might spend a lot more time with them than usual.

April is full of happy events – you might be a desired guest at parties, where you are able to be your very best. You are likely to meet new people, which is a good thing if you are single or your relationship has already run its course.

Your relationship with relatives has been a bit rocky in the recent past, and in April things will become more predictable. Even if you have not resolved everything, it's better than nothing. And remember, there is no such thing as bad peace or a good war.

Health. In April, you are feeling energetic and have no reason to fear any illness. April is also a great time to overhaul your wardrobe, change up your image, or undergo any cosmetic procedures.

May

New York Time			London Time		
Calendar Day	Lunar Day	Lunar Day Start Time	Calendar Day	Lunar Day	Lunar Day Start Time
01/05/2022	2	6:18 AM	01/05/2022	2	5:48 AM
02/05/2022	3	6:53 AM	02/05/2022	3	6:14 AM
03/05/2022	4	7:32 AM	03/05/2022	4	6:47 AM
04/05/2022	5	8:16 AM	04/05/2022	5	7:27 AM
05/05/2022	6	9:06 AM	05/05/2022	6	8:14 AM
06/05/2022	7	10:00 AM	06/05/2022	7	9:10 AM
07/05/2022	8	10:57 AM	07/05/2022	8	10:12 AM
08/05/2022	9	11:57 AM	08/05/2022	9	11:18 AM
09/05/2022	10	12:59 PM	09/05/2022	10	12:27 PM
10/05/2022	11	2:02 PM	10/05/2022	11	1:38 PM
11/05/2022	12	3:06 PM	11/05/2022	12	2:51 PM
12/05/2022	13	4:13 PM	12/05/2022	13	4:07 PM
13/05/2022	14	5:22 PM	13/05/2022	14	5:25 PM
14/05/2022	15	6:34 PM	14/05/2022	15	6:47 PM
15/05/2022	16	7:49 PM	15/05/2022	16	8:11 PM
16/05/2022	17	9:03 PM	16/05/2022	17	9:34 PM
17/05/2022	18	10:14 PM	17/05/2022	18	10:50 PM
18/05/2022	19	11:16 PM	18/05/2022	19	11:55 PM
20/05/2022	20	12:10 AM	20/05/2022	20	12:46 AM
21/05/2022	21	12:53 AM	21/05/2022	21	1:24 AM
22/05/2022	22	1:30 AM	22/05/2022	22	1:53 AM
23/05/2022	23	2:01 AM	23/05/2022	23	2:16 AM
24/05/2022	24	2:30 AM	24/05/2022	24	2:36 AM
25/05/2022	25	2:56 AM	25/05/2022	25	2:54 AM
26/05/2022	26	3:23 AM	26/05/2022	26	3:12 AM
27/05/2022	27	3:50 AM	27/05/2022	27	3:31 AM
28/05/2022	28	4:20 AM	28/05/2022	28	3:52 AM
29/05/2022	29	4:53 AM	29/05/2022	29	4:17 AM
30/05/2022	30	5:30 AM	30/05/2022	30	4:47 AM
30/05/2022	1	7:32 AM	30/05/2022	1	12:32 PM
31/05/2022	2	6:13 AM	31/05/2022	2	5:24 AM

You can find the description of each lunar day in the chapter "A Guide to The Moon Cycle and Lunar Days"

In May, you are so active that even your loved ones who are used to you are surprised. You are in constant motion, and making strides. But after all, you're a Sagittarius!

Work. May is a month of activity and hard work. You have some new tasks at hand, and you might end up so absorbed in it all that even if you take vacation time in May, you will spend the whole time either working or thinking about work!

Because of the way you are tackling business, unfinished tasks that seemed impossible to finish will either fade into the background or somehow end up settled.

Your relationship with colleagues from other cities or abroad will look calmer this month. You may occasionally see problems from the past reappearing, but you know what to do by now, so you are able to handle things.

The best time for anything work-related is the first ten days of May. This is the best time to plan any major events or meetings. From May 10 to June 3, Mercury will be in retrograde, which will lead to some setbacks at work, the people you need being absent, and red tape.

This is a time to sit back and really focus on what you need to do while making any necessary adjustments. Be patient – later, you will be able to keep moving forward with things. If you are sure that you can handle it and you have enough time, maybe take some time off to relax.

Money. May is a great time for your finances. You will be receiving regular income, and significantly more of it, too. In addition to your usual salary, you can count on additional profits from various real estate transactions. You can also expect support from parents or loved ones.

Love and family. Your personal life is also abuzz with activity, this month. Most likely, you are busy building a home, remodeling your apartment, and all of this toil and trouble is finally coming to a blissful end.

Your children are a source of joy, and they are starting a new, much happier and favorable period, which you will start to notice very soon.

Single people are starting a new, exciting period, as well. You can expect new love, which will leave you feeling very content. The luckiest Sagittarians will see this happen in May, while others will have to wait until the summer of 2022.

Health. In May, you are not feeling particularly energetic, so try to find the time to relax, and if you can't, at least get enough sleep, and spend some time in nature on the weekends.

June

New York Time			London Time		
Calendar Day	Lunar Day	Lunar Day Start Time	Calendar Day	Lunar Day	Lunar Day Start Time
01/06/2022	3	7:00 AM	01/06/2022	3	6:09 AM
02/06/2022	4	7:53 AM	02/06/2022	4	7:02 AM
03/06/2022	5	8:49 AM	03/06/2022	5	8:02 AM
04/06/2022	6	9:48 AM	04/06/2022	6	9:06 AM
05/06/2022	7	10:48 AM	05/06/2022	7	10:14 AM
06/06/2022	8	11:49 AM	06/06/2022	8	11:23 AM
07/06/2022	9	12:51 PM	07/06/2022	9	12:33 PM
08/06/2022	10	1:55 PM	08/06/2022	10	1:45 PM
09/06/2022	11	3:01 PM	09/06/2022	11	3:00 PM
10/06/2022	12	4:10 PM	10/06/2022	12	4:18 PM
11/06/2022	13	5:22 PM	11/06/2022	13	5:39 PM
12/06/2022	14	6:37 PM	12/06/2022	14	7:03 PM
13/06/2022	15	7:50 PM	13/06/2022	15	8:24 PM
14/06/2022	16	8:58 PM	14/06/2022	16	9:36 PM
15/06/2022	17	9:58 PM	15/06/2022	17	10:35 PM
16/06/2022	18	10:47 PM	16/06/2022	18	11:20 PM
17/06/2022	19	11:28 PM	17/06/2022	19	11:54 PM
19/06/2022	20	12:03 AM	19/06/2022	20	12:20 AM
20/06/2022	21	12:33 AM	20/06/2022	21	12:42 AM
21/06/2022	22	1:00 AM	21/06/2022	22	1:01 AM
22/06/2022	23	1:27 AM	22/06/2022	23	1:19 AM
23/06/2022	24	1:54 AM	23/06/2022	24	1:38 AM
24/06/2022	25	2:23 AM	24/06/2022	25	1:58 AM
25/06/2022	26	2:54 AM	25/06/2022	26	2:21 AM
26/06/2022	27	3:30 AM	26/06/2022	27	2:49 AM
27/06/2022	28	4:11 AM	27/06/2022	28	3:24 AM
28/06/2022	29	4:57 AM	28/06/2022	29	4:06 AM
28/06/2022	1	10:53 PM	29/06/2022	1	3:53 AM
29/06/2022	2	5:48 AM	29/06/2022	2	4:56 AM
30/06/2022	3	6:43 AM	30/06/2022	3	5:54 AM

You can find the description of each lunar day in the chapter "A Guide to The Moon Cycle and Lunar Days"

Your life is changing and becoming more interesting, easier, and fun. You have worked a lot, and now, just like Cinderella, it's your chance to go to the ball.

Work. June is a great time for you at work. Entrepreneurs and managers will finish up some projects that have been keeping you busy, and might think about a new start. This may involve reconsidering your staff and hire some new colleagues. They will be reliable and helpful in many areas.

Employees might begin negotiating a raise, this will turn out well for you. Alternatively, you might receive a job offer in a new, more promising company.

Your connections with others will be another positive side of June. You will have new partners and an inspiring relationship with your current colleagues, which will be easy, natural, and naturally good-willed. You will prove yourself a skilled negotiator and capable of convincing anyone of anything.

You will also begin connecting more with colleagues from other cities or abroad, and might go on a successful trip.

Money. When it comes to money, June is a lucky time for you. You will see great opportunities to improve your financial situation, and this is the case for all Sagittarians, regardless of your field. You might get a raise, bonus, or profits from projects you completed earlier, or partial payment for new ideas. Expect the largest sums on June 6-8, 13, 14, 24, and 25.

Love and family. June is a good time for your personal life, too. If you have a family, the most important events this month will involve your children, who are healthy and behaving well if they are small, and finally on the right path toward prosperity and development if they are already grown up.

Most Sagittarians can expect success and attention all month long. You will be surrounded by a lot of people, and attend a lot of events, parties, and other celebrations. So, if you are aiming for stardom, now is the time!

If you are feeling in the mood for romance, you can count on new acquaintances, and an exciting romance with an unpredictable end. This is great for single people, but it will complicate your life if you already have a long-term partner. The ball is in your court, and the stars will offer you their advice, but how things end is up to you. You might go on a trip which will be very successful and expand your social circle.

Health. In June, you are energetic, witty, and incredibly sexually attractive. You might feel a little less confident at the end of the month, during the new moon on June 29 and 30. During these days, you might feel tired from work, meetings, and dealing with others. In July, you can finally relax and actually enjoy the calm.

July

New York Time			London Time		
Calendar Day	Lunar Day	Lunar Day Start Time	Calendar Day	Lunar Day	Lunar Day Start Time
01/07/2022	4	7:41 AM	01/07/2022	4	6:57 AM
02/07/2022	5	8:41 AM	02/07/2022	5	8:04 AM
03/07/2022	6	9:41 AM	03/07/2022	6	9:12 AM
04/07/2022	7	10:42 AM	04/07/2022	7	10:22 AM
05/07/2022	8	11:44 AM	05/07/2022	8	11:32 AM
06/07/2022	9	12:47 PM	06/07/2022	9	12:44 PM
07/07/2022	10	1:53 PM	07/07/2022	10	1:58 PM
08/07/2022	11	3:01 PM	08/07/2022	11	3:15 PM
09/07/2022	12	4:13 PM	09/07/2022	12	4:35 PM
10/07/2022	13	5:25 PM	10/07/2022	13	5:56 PM
11/07/2022	14	6:35 PM	11/07/2022	14	7:12 PM
12/07/2022	15	7:40 PM	12/07/2022	15	8:18 PM
13/07/2022	16	8:35 PM	13/07/2022	16	9:10 PM
14/07/2022	17	9:21 PM	14/07/2022	17	9:50 PM
15/07/2022	18	9:59 PM	15/07/2022	18	10:20 PM
16/07/2022	19	10:32 PM	16/07/2022	19	10:45 PM
17/07/2022	20	11:02 PM	17/07/2022	20	11:05 PM
18/07/2022	21	11:29 PM	18/07/2022	21	11:25 PM
19/07/2022	22	11:57 PM	19/07/2022	22	11:43 PM
21/07/2022	23	12:25 AM	21/07/2022	23	12:03 AM
22/07/2022	24	12:56 AM	22/07/2022	24	12:26 AM
23/07/2022	25	1:31 AM	23/07/2022	25	12:52 AM
24/07/2022	26	2:10 AM	24/07/2022	26	1:25 AM
25/07/2022	27	2:54 AM	25/07/2022	27	2:04 AM
26/07/2022	28	3:43 AM	26/07/2022	28	2:52 AM
27/07/2022	29	4:37 AM	27/07/2022	29	3:47 AM
28/07/2022	30	5:35 AM	28/07/2022	30	4:49 AM
28/07/2022	1	1:55 PM	28/07/2022	1	6:55 PM
29/07/2022	2	6:34 AM	29/07/2022	2	5:55 AM
30/07/2022	3	7:35 AM	30/07/2022	3	7:04 AM
31/07/2022	4	8:36 AM	31/07/2022	4	8:13 AM

You can find the description of each lunar day in the chapter "A Guide to The Moon Cycle and Lunar Days"

July is a time for you to catch your breath between a turbulent, jam-packed June and what's going to be an active, dynamic August. Remember there's more to life than working, and act accordingly.

Work. In June, most Sagittarians would rather focus their energy on their families and personal matters than work-related responsibilities. Only the most incurable workaholics will be busy getting their business in order and dealing with administrative issues.

Entrepreneurs and managers are thinking about hiring new employees, as the stars are suggesting that your current staffing leaves a lot to be desired.

Employees who are still at work might have trouble dividing time between their personal and professional obligations. The stars recommend that you take a few days off and focus your energy where you really want to.

July is a good time to establish connections with colleagues and friends living in other cities or abroad. Perhaps one of them will remind you this month.

Money. July is not the best month for you, financially speaking. All month long, you will be spending money rather than making it. The astrologist predicts that many of your expenses in July will be either pleasant or practical, and related to your personal life, including family and your children's needs. However, you can count on the largest amounts coming in on July 4, 5, 13, 21, 22, and 31.

Love and family. Expect some real achievements in your personal life. Couples who get along will support their children, who are now on the path to prosperity and success. Some families may even be welcoming new members.

Your relationship with relatives is significantly better than it was, and a family member may come visit you.

When it comes to romance, you have had smooth sailing for a while, now. Your relationship is growing deeper and becoming warmer and more serious. If for some time it has seemed that you are on the same plane, right now, things are somewhat different, and this summer is likely to reveal the exact opposite.

Health. Some trouble lies ahead in July: your home and job are demanding your attention. Weekends out of the city, spending time in the woods or in a nearby park are a way to get away from the constant frenzy, but also good for the body and soul.

The stars also strongly urge you to be careful with your eating habits and avoid eating anything questionable. Generally speaking, a healthy diet will prevent a lot of problems, especially if you have issues with your weight or chronic digestive conditions.

August

New York Time				London Time		
Calendar Day	Lunar Day	Lunar Day Start Time		Calendar Day	Lunar Day	Lunar Day Start Time
01/08/2022	5	9:37 AM		01/08/2022	5	9:23 AM
02/08/2022	6	10:40 AM		02/08/2022	6	10:34 AM
03/08/2022	7	11:44 AM		03/08/2022	7	11:46 AM
04/08/2022	8	12:49 PM		04/08/2022	8	1:00 PM
05/08/2022	9	1:58 PM		05/08/2022	9	2:17 PM
06/08/2022	10	3:07 PM		06/08/2022	10	3:35 PM
07/08/2022	11	4:16 PM		07/08/2022	11	4:51 PM
08/08/2022	12	5:22 PM		08/08/2022	12	6:00 PM
09/08/2022	13	6:20 PM		09/08/2022	13	6:58 PM
10/08/2022	14	7:10 PM		10/08/2022	14	7:43 PM
11/08/2022	15	7:52 PM		11/08/2022	15	8:17 PM
12/08/2022	16	8:28 PM		12/08/2022	16	8:45 PM
13/08/2022	17	9:00 PM		13/08/2022	17	9:07 PM
14/08/2022	18	9:29 PM		14/08/2022	18	9:28 PM
15/08/2022	19	9:57 PM		15/08/2022	19	9:47 PM
16/08/2022	20	10:26 PM		16/08/2022	20	10:07 PM
17/08/2022	21	10:56 PM		17/08/2022	21	10:29 PM
18/08/2022	22	11:30 PM		18/08/2022	22	10:54 PM
20/08/2022	23	12:08 AM		19/08/2022	23	11:25 PM
21/08/2022	24	12:50 AM		21/08/2022	24	12:02 AM
22/08/2022	25	1:38 AM		22/08/2022	25	12:46 AM
23/08/2022	26	2:30 AM		23/08/2022	26	1:39 AM
24/08/2022	27	3:27 AM		24/08/2022	27	2:39 AM
25/08/2022	28	4:26 AM		25/08/2022	28	3:45 AM
26/08/2022	29	5:27 AM		26/08/2022	29	4:53 AM
27/08/2022	1	4:16 AM		27/08/2022	30	6:02 AM
27/08/2022	2	6:28 AM		27/08/2022	1	9:16 AM
28/08/2022	3	7:30 AM		28/08/2022	2	7:13 AM
29/08/2022	4	8:33 AM		29/08/2022	3	8:24 AM
30/08/2022	5	9:37 AM		30/08/2022	4	9:36 AM
31/08/2022	6	10:42 AM		31/08/2022	5	10:50 AM

You can find the description of each lunar day in the chapter "A Guide to The Moon Cycle and Lunar Days"

All month long, you will be striving to reach new heights. This is a long, winding road, but it is a steep and toilsome way to the stars!

Work. This is a very busy time for you at work, and a very successful time, too. During the first ten days of the month, you may go on a trip, and you may be working on plans with colleagues from faraway. Everything should go as planned, though you may experience some unexpected disagreements along the way. They may look differently, depending on your field and future plans. In some cases, there may be issues with laws in another country, and in others, your own flaws will come out unexpectedly, right at a crucial moment.

Entrepreneurs and managers should be more careful when dealing with subordinates and meticulously check their work. Any errors might significantly set back your plans – keep that in mind and act accordingly.

The most difficult time for this is August 5-7 and 12 and 13. If you face any kind of obstacles, remember that in any case, you are moving ahead, so keep your eye on the prize and don't leave your chosen path.

Employees should be careful when dealing with colleagues and at any team-related events. In case of conflict, take no sides, and take pains to avoid any intrigue.

For all Sagittarians, it is important to avoid breaking any laws and to carefully prepare for any traveling, which is highly likely during various periods this month.

Money. Your finances are looking rather neutral this month, though the first few days of the month you can expect some gifts from Fate. Overall, however, you will not run into any major windfalls, though your expenses will remain modest. Expect the largest sums to come in on August 1, 2, 9, 10, 17-19, and 27-29.

Love and family. If your interests are focused on your family life, here you can expect several developments of various natures.

Things are moving along well for couples, whose relationship is growing and bringing them closer together. They might spend some time traveling together or on vacation, though it is worth carefully preparing for that, in order to avoid any unpleasant surprises.

In many families, you will continue to see positive changes related to children, though this will still require attention and money on your part. Of course, children are something sacred, and who, if not you?

Spouses who are dealing with a mountain of issues will run into a rocky period, and your relationship will feel pressure from the heavens. Mars, an active and aggressive planet will move into the sector of the sky related to long-term partners on August 20, and remain there for six months. Be prepared to tackle this event head on and consider any weak links in your relationship. That is the best you can do.

You might also face further trouble this month, in the form of unexpected problems involving your own family members. What that looks like may change depending on the person, and while you can't make any predictions, you can expect some turbulence. Most likely, this will involve old problems rearing their heads again, and looking more acute than they were.

Health. In August, you are energetic, though the stars urge you to be careful when traveling or driving. There is a danger of accidents, which is especially high on August 5-7, 12, 13, and 25-28. Be careful! These are days to watch out for!

September

New York Time			London Time		
Calendar Day	Lunar Day	Lunar Day Start Time	Calendar Day	Lunar Day	Lunar Day Start Time
01/09/2022	7	11:49 AM	01/09/2022	6	12:06 PM
02/09/2022	8	12:57 PM	02/09/2022	7	1:23 PM
03/09/2022	9	2:05 PM	03/09/2022	8	2:38 PM
04/09/2022	10	3:10 PM	04/09/2022	9	3:48 PM
05/09/2022	11	4:10 PM	05/09/2022	10	4:48 PM
06/09/2022	12	5:01 PM	06/09/2022	11	5:37 PM
07/09/2022	13	5:45 PM	07/09/2022	12	6:14 PM
08/09/2022	14	6:23 PM	08/09/2022	13	6:44 PM
09/09/2022	15	6:56 PM	09/09/2022	14	7:08 PM
10/09/2022	16	7:26 PM	10/09/2022	15	7:30 PM
11/09/2022	17	7:55 PM	11/09/2022	16	7:50 PM
12/09/2022	18	8:24 PM	12/09/2022	17	8:10 PM
13/09/2022	19	8:54 PM	13/09/2022	18	8:31 PM
14/09/2022	20	9:27 PM	14/09/2022	19	8:55 PM
15/09/2022	21	10:04 PM	15/09/2022	20	9:24 PM
16/09/2022	22	10:45 PM	16/09/2022	21	9:58 PM
17/09/2022	23	11:31 PM	17/09/2022	22	10:40 PM
19/09/2022	24	12:22 AM	18/09/2022	23	11:30 PM
20/09/2022	25	1:17 AM	20/09/2022	24	12:28 AM
21/09/2022	26	2:15 AM	21/09/2022	25	1:31 AM
22/09/2022	27	3:15 AM	22/09/2022	26	2:38 AM
23/09/2022	28	4:17 AM	23/09/2022	27	3:47 AM
24/09/2022	29	5:19 AM	24/09/2022	28	4:58 AM
25/09/2022	30	6:22 AM	25/09/2022	29	6:10 AM
25/09/2022	1	5:54 PM	25/09/2022	1	10:54 PM
26/09/2022	2	7:27 AM	26/09/2022	2	7:23 AM
27/09/2022	3	8:33 AM	27/09/2022	3	8:38 AM
28/09/2022	4	9:40 AM	28/09/2022	4	9:54 AM
29/09/2022	5	10:49 AM	29/09/2022	5	11:12 AM
30/09/2022	6	11:58 AM	30/09/2022	6	12:29 PM

You can find the description of each lunar day in the chapter "A Guide to The Moon Cycle and Lunar Days"

In theory, September could be one of the best months of 2022 for you – everything you need is right there. But every rose has its thorn, and you might be dealing with a lot of thorns, right now.

Work. In September, you may find yourself very busy at work, and during the first 10 days of the month you will be very productive, too. From September 10 to October 2, however, Mercury, the planet responsible for connections and contacts, will be in retrograde, and you will realize that it is suddenly very difficult to move forward with anything (in the best of cases), if not impossible.

Many Sagittarians will be grappling with problems involving a friend or someone highly placed who once provided you with great support.

You will also feel a lot of tension with other people, and that may take on the form of unfriendly competition. Though you are in a strong position, be careful, as this situation is unlikely to end anytime soon. Competitors are not going to retreat, and they will begin making one demand after the next. It is worth taking this into consideration. In September, your negotiations with them will not go very far, and this is unlikely to be resolved for the next three to four months.

Money. Despite all the trouble at work, everything is looking good when it comes to your finances. You might receive a nice profit from some work you completed in the past, and you can expect the greatest sums to come in on September 5-7, 14, 15, and 25-27. You will have a lot of expenses, and they may be related to your work-related issues, or possibly your personal life.

Love and family. If, by the will of Fate, most of your excitement this month will happen in your personal life, peace and quiet is still only a dream.

In many families, you are experiencing disagreements with your children. The elder generation may be worried about various collisions between your personal and professional lives, while younger family members' behavior may leave much to be desired. Alternatively, your children's needs may require a huge amount of money and the entire family will feel the weight of that burden.

This will be a hard month for couples, as they will have to unexpectedly change their plans due to the emergence of new tasks and plans.

You will have to have a serious talk with a loved one in mid-September, and this may shed a lot of light on your relationship. This may allow both of you to better understand each other's nature. That is a good thing, as long as it allows you to move forward in understanding what is going on around you. Alternatively, your partner's position may be difficult for you to accept. If there is any love between you, you should be able to find some sort of compromise.

Married couples might also find themselves arguing. During the second half of the month, you might face unexpected complaints you may not have an answer for. Your arguing and conflict may continue through the rest of 2022, which will seriously weaken your family ties and force you to look at your relationship from a new perspective. Remember that and try to nip any fights in the bud, so they don't turn into an all-out forest fire.

Health. In September, you are feeling energetic, which means you are able to take on anything this month throws at you.

October

New York Time				London Time		
Calendar Day	Lunar Day	Lunar Day Start Time		Calendar Day	Lunar Day	Lunar Day Start Time
01/10/2022	7	1:04 PM		01/10/2022	7	1:41 PM
02/10/2022	8	2:04 PM		02/10/2022	8	2:44 PM
03/10/2022	9	2:57 PM		03/10/2022	9	3:35 PM
04/10/2022	10	3:43 PM		04/10/2022	10	4:15 PM
05/10/2022	11	4:21 PM		05/10/2022	11	4:46 PM
06/10/2022	12	4:55 PM		06/10/2022	12	5:11 PM
07/10/2022	13	5:25 PM		07/10/2022	13	5:33 PM
08/10/2022	14	5:54 PM		08/10/2022	14	5:53 PM
09/10/2022	15	6:23 PM		09/10/2022	15	6:12 PM
10/10/2022	16	6:52 PM		10/10/2022	16	6:33 PM
11/10/2022	17	7:24 PM		11/10/2022	17	6:55 PM
12/10/2022	18	7:59 PM		12/10/2022	18	7:22 PM
13/10/2022	19	8:39 PM		13/10/2022	19	7:54 PM
14/10/2022	20	9:23 PM		14/10/2022	20	8:34 PM
15/10/2022	21	10:12 PM		15/10/2022	21	9:21 PM
16/10/2022	22	11:06 PM		16/10/2022	22	10:16 PM
18/10/2022	23	12:03 AM		17/10/2022	23	11:17 PM
19/10/2022	24	1:02 AM		19/10/2022	24	12:22 AM
20/10/2022	25	2:03 AM		20/10/2022	25	1:30 AM
21/10/2022	26	3:04 AM		21/10/2022	26	2:39 AM
22/10/2022	27	4:06 AM		22/10/2022	27	3:50 AM
23/10/2022	28	5:10 AM		23/10/2022	28	5:03 AM
24/10/2022	29	6:16 AM		24/10/2022	29	6:18 AM
25/10/2022	1	6:48 AM		25/10/2022	30	7:35 AM
25/10/2022	2	7:25 AM		25/10/2022	1	11:48 AM
26/10/2022	3	8:35 AM		26/10/2022	2	8:54 AM
27/10/2022	4	9:46 AM		27/10/2022	3	10:14 AM
28/10/2022	5	10:55 AM		28/10/2022	4	11:30 AM
29/10/2022	6	11:59 AM		29/10/2022	5	12:38 PM
30/10/2022	7	12:55 PM		30/10/2022	6	12:33 PM
31/10/2022	8	1:42 PM		31/10/2022	7	1:16 PM

You can find the description of each lunar day in the chapter "A Guide to The Moon Cycle and Lunar Days"

You are looking at an unusually successful month, in which you will literally be able to climb mountains. Your inherent optimism may sometimes simply shoot off the charts, and turn into risky adventurism. Be careful!

Work. October is a good time to hold onto your position and shake off some of the debris accumulated in the past. You will be adventurous, bold, and capable of drawing both friends and highly placed people to your business. You will also be able to easily resolve issues that require the goodwill of official authorities.

Entrepreneurs and managers will be able to continue work that had stalled in September. Your difficult relationship with a partner has been bothering you since last month, but things are looking up, though the future will reveal that things are still not stable. In October, however, you will have help from like-minded friends and someone highly placed, who will act as an intermediary and improve things significantly.

In this case, the astrologist suggests backing up any agreements with something tangible, like a signed contract. If your partners start to waver later on, then you will avoid a lot of headaches.

Employees are on a lucky streak at work, and management is taking notice of your efforts, as is someone highly placed.

Any business trips planned for October will go well, and make it possible to fix your relationship with a former colleague, as well as old friends.

Money. This month, your financial situation is looking good. You might find money you had forgotten about, or profits from your hard work in the past. Your expenses in October will be pleasant – shopping, going out with friends, and your loved ones' needs.

Love and family. October is a good time for your personal life, too. Your circle of friends is growing, and you are often visiting friends at gatherings, parties, events, and you are able to leave a favorable impression on anyone Fate places in your path. For single people, this is a great time to meet someone.

Spouses with a strong marriage will come back to some issues from the past as the month draws to a close. This will be related to fixing up a summer home, apartment, or a new home.

For those whose relationship leaves something to be desired, you may reach a truce, though it will be fragile and somewhat unreliable. But remember that bad peace is better than a good war, at least for some people ☺ Most likely, if there are any thorny material or moral issues, they will be resolved closer to mid-October.

Health. For most of October, you will be feeling energetic and have no reason to fear falling ill. However, during the new moon and eclipse, on October 25-27, you might feel a bit more sluggish. These are the most difficult days in October, so be sure to stay calm and avoid any risky situations.

November

New York Time			London Time		
Calendar Day	Lunar Day	Lunar Day Start Time	Calendar Day	Lunar Day	Lunar Day Start Time
01/11/2022	9	2:23 PM	01/11/2022	8	1:50 PM
02/11/2022	10	2:57 PM	02/11/2022	9	2:16 PM
03/11/2022	11	3:27 PM	03/11/2022	10	2:38 PM
04/11/2022	12	3:56 PM	04/11/2022	11	2:58 PM
05/11/2022	13	4:24 PM	05/11/2022	12	3:17 PM
06/11/2022	14	3:52 PM	06/11/2022	13	3:36 PM
07/11/2022	15	4:22 PM	07/11/2022	14	3:58 PM
08/11/2022	16	4:56 PM	08/11/2022	15	4:22 PM
09/11/2022	17	5:33 PM	09/11/2022	16	4:52 PM
10/11/2022	18	6:16 PM	10/11/2022	17	5:28 PM
11/11/2022	19	7:04 PM	11/11/2022	18	6:12 PM
12/11/2022	20	7:56 PM	12/11/2022	19	7:05 PM
13/11/2022	21	8:52 PM	13/11/2022	20	8:03 PM
14/11/2022	22	9:50 PM	14/11/2022	21	9:07 PM
15/11/2022	23	10:49 PM	15/11/2022	22	10:13 PM
16/11/2022	24	11:49 PM	16/11/2022	23	11:21 PM
18/11/2022	25	12:50 AM	18/11/2022	24	12:30 AM
19/11/2022	26	1:52 AM	19/11/2022	25	1:41 AM
20/11/2022	27	2:56 AM	20/11/2022	26	2:53 AM
21/11/2022	28	4:03 AM	21/11/2022	27	4:09 AM
22/11/2022	29	5:13 AM	22/11/2022	28	5:27 AM
23/11/2022	30	6:25 AM	23/11/2022	29	6:48 AM
23/11/2022	1	5:57 PM	23/11/2022	1	10:57 PM
24/11/2022	2	7:37 AM	24/11/2022	2	8:08 AM
25/11/2022	3	8:45 AM	25/11/2022	3	9:23 AM
26/11/2022	4	9:47 AM	26/11/2022	4	10:25 AM
27/11/2022	5	10:39 AM	27/11/2022	5	11:15 AM
28/11/2022	6	11:23 AM	28/11/2022	6	11:52 AM
29/11/2022	7	12:00 PM	29/11/2022	7	12:21 PM
30/11/2022	8	12:31 PM	30/11/2022	8	12:45 PM

You can find the description of each lunar day in the chapter "A Guide to The Moon Cycle and Lunar Days"

Traditionally, November is a stressful month for you. That goes for this year, too, so stay on your toes, keep a cool head, and act carefully and with restraint.

Work. This is not exactly a good time for you at work. Entrepreneurs and managers at every level will face a whole host of problems.

Your relationships with colleagues in other cities and abroad have once again hit a wall. You may see breaches of previous agreements or new obstacles you will have to take into consideration.

Pay close attention to your associates – they may disappoint you. This is an area you have had to take a look at for some time, so it is worth coming up with a clear plan and shaking things up.

Many Sagittarians may come back to issues related to real estate. Those planning on expanding their business will have to add something or make changes. There is, however, hope that by New Year's, all of these administrative plans will be resolved, and in your favor.

Employees should keep an eye on colleagues. This month, you may run into some covert activities working against you, which will undermine your professional position and reputation.

Money. Financially, November might look differently. Some Sagittarians will receive payment from a previously completed job, while others will take on credit. You might profit from various real estate transactions, as well as receive financial support from a business partner.

Those who are not part of the business world can count on help from parents, a spouse, or loved ones. In sum, despite the stormy waters at work, you will not find yourself penniless.

Love and family. Many Sagittarians will be immersed in home improvements in November. You might be putting the finishing touches on your apartment, home, or summer home.

In more modest cases, you may be finishing major repairs. This may lead to spats between spouses, which is only natural when you are going through such bothersome, tedious tasks.

Your relationship with a relative will once again become difficult. You can expect serious conflicts in the first half of November, but this is nothing new – for the umpteenth time, you are seeing unresolved problems resurface. It may involve longstanding arguments, or support for a relative going through hard times.

For couples, November is a very difficult time. You might see information revealed that both parties would prefer to have kept secret. This will seriously damage your relationship, and in the most severe cases, it will lead to a separation. At the very least, you can expect a serious fight.

You know best what is important to you, and what you are willing to accept. What's more, you know what your deal breakers are.

Health. Take care of yourself, as November is sure to lead to the reemergence of old diseases, or possibly new ones. Be careful when traveling and behind the wheel. The first half of the month is especially critical, here. The 6th through 13th of November are the riskiest days of the month.

December

New York Time				London Time		
Calendar Day	Lunar Day	Lunar Day Start Time		Calendar Day	Lunar Day	Lunar Day Start Time
01/12/2022	9	1:00 PM		01/12/2022	9	1:05 PM
02/12/2022	10	1:27 PM		02/12/2022	10	1:24 PM
03/12/2022	11	1:55 PM		03/12/2022	11	1:42 PM
04/12/2022	12	2:24 PM		04/12/2022	12	2:03 PM
05/12/2022	13	2:56 PM		05/12/2022	13	2:25 PM
06/12/2022	14	3:31 PM		06/12/2022	14	2:53 PM
07/12/2022	15	4:11 PM		07/12/2022	15	3:26 PM
08/12/2022	16	4:57 PM		08/12/2022	16	4:07 PM
09/12/2022	17	5:48 PM		09/12/2022	17	4:56 PM
10/12/2022	18	6:42 PM		10/12/2022	18	5:53 PM
11/12/2022	19	7:40 PM		11/12/2022	19	6:55 PM
12/12/2022	20	8:39 PM		12/12/2022	20	8:00 PM
13/12/2022	21	9:38 PM		13/12/2022	21	9:07 PM
14/12/2022	22	10:37 PM		14/12/2022	22	10:15 PM
15/12/2022	23	11:37 PM		15/12/2022	23	11:23 PM
17/12/2022	24	12:39 AM		17/12/2022	24	12:32 AM
18/12/2022	25	1:42 AM		18/12/2022	25	1:44 AM
19/12/2022	26	2:49 AM		19/12/2022	26	2:59 AM
20/12/2022	27	3:58 AM		20/12/2022	27	4:18 AM
21/12/2022	28	5:10 AM		21/12/2022	28	5:38 AM
22/12/2022	29	6:22 AM		22/12/2022	29	6:56 AM
23/12/2022	1	5:17 AM		23/12/2022	30	8:07 AM
23/12/2022	2	7:28 AM		23/12/2022	1	10:17 AM
24/12/2022	3	8:27 AM		24/12/2022	2	9:04 AM
25/12/2022	4	9:17 AM		25/12/2022	3	9:49 AM
26/12/2022	5	9:58 AM		26/12/2022	4	10:22 AM
27/12/2022	6	10:32 AM		27/12/2022	5	10:49 AM
28/12/2022	7	11:03 AM		28/12/2022	6	11:11 AM
29/12/2022	8	11:31 AM		29/12/2022	7	11:30 AM
30/12/2022	9	11:59 AM		30/12/2022	8	11:49 AM
31/12/2022	10	12:28 PM		31/12/2022	9	12:09 PM

You can find the description of each lunar day in the chapter "A Guide to The Moon Cycle and Lunar Days"

In December, you will be bold, persistent, and a bit of an adventurer. In an eternal battle, we only dream of peace!

Work. In December, many Sagittarians will have to come back to issues from the recent past. Most likely, this involves land, real estate, or other major property, and both you and your partners will have differing views on how it should be used and who owns it.

Regardless of what happens in your case, it is impossible to predict how things will turn out, but one thing is clear – the underlying cause of this problem is in the past, and everyone has one. This situation will continue until late December, when you might be able to find an acceptable solution for both parties.

Your connections to colleagues in other cities or abroad are moving along nicely. Old friends might act as intermediaries in case of any difficulties with stubborn opponents.

Money. Despite the ups and downs this month at work, overall, your finances will be unscathed. You will have regular income, and that is especially noticeable closer to the end of December. Expect the largest sums to come in on December 5, 6, 13-15, and 23-25.

Love and family. In many cases, you are focused on your personal life more than work this month. You might have conflicts on your hands, no matter how well your family gets along, and the cause is most likely various issues related to your home.

Couples who are on the rocks might be closer than ever to divorce in December, and that situation is likely to become extremely tense. A close relative might be the link who brings warring spouses together.

In some families, you may deal with problems related to your parents. That may involve a serious argument, or possibly an illness or other problems that may afflict the elder members of your family.

Generally speaking, life is not exactly calm right now, and things start to look a little more peaceful toward the end of the month.

Health. All month long, you will feel cheerful and confident. That means you are able to resolve a lot of problems this month, and take a bold look toward the future and 2023.

A guide to the Moon cycle and Lunar days

Since Ancient times, people have noticed that the moon has a strong influence on nature. Our Earth and everything living on it is a single living being, which is why the phases of the moon have such an effect on our health and mental state, and therefore, our lives. Remember Shakespeare and his description of Othello's jealousy in his famous tragedy:

"It is the very error of the moon, She comes more nearer Earth than she was wont And makes men mad."

If our inner rhythm is in harmony with that of the cosmos, we are able to achieve much more. People were aware of this a thousand years ago. The lunar calendar is ancient. We can find it among the ancient Sumerians (4000-3000 BC), the inhabitants of Mesopotamia, Native Americans, Hindus, and ancient Slavs. There is evidence that the Siberian Yakuts had a lunar calendar, as did the Malaysians.

Primitive tribes saw the moon as a source of fertility. Long before Christianity, the waxing moon was seen as favorable for planting new crops and starting a new business, for success and making money, while the waning moon was a sign that business would end.

1   2   3   4   5   6   7   8

What are the phases of the moon?

- Phase 1 – new moon
- Phase 2 – waxing crescent moon
- Phase 3 – first quarter moon
- Phase 4 – waxing gibbous moon
- Phase 5 – full moon
- Phase 6 – waning gibbous moon
- Phase 7 – third quarter moon
- Phase 8 – waning crescent moon

To simplify things, we can divide the month into two phases:
Waxing crescent moon - before the full moon
Waning crescent moon - after the full moon

New Moon

We cannot see the new moon, as it is hidden. People might complain about feeling weak, mental imbalance, and fatigue. During this time, we want to avoid taking on too much or overdoing things. Generally, people are not very responsive and react poorly to requests, which is why it is best to look out for yourself, while not keeping your plate too full.

The new moon is a bad time for advertising – it will go unnoticed. It is not worth preparing any presentations, parties, or loud gatherings. People are feeling constrained, not very social, and sluggish.

This is also a less than ideal time for surgery, as your recovery will be slow, and the likelihood of medical error is high.

It is also difficult to get an accurate diagnosis during the new moon – diseases might seem to be hidden, and doctors might not see the real underlying cause of what ails you.

The new moon is also a bad time for dates, and sexual encounters may be dissatisfying and leave you feeling disappointed. Ancient astrologers did not advise planning a wedding night during the new moon.

Waxing Crescent Moon

It is easy to identify a waxing crescent moon. If you draw an imaginary line between the two "horns", you should see the letter P. The waxing moon is then divided into one and two quarters.

During the first quarter moon, we need to focus on planning – setting goals and thinking of how we will set about achieving them. However, it is still a good idea to hold back a bit and not overdo things. Energy levels are still low, though they are growing along with the moon. It is still a good idea to avoid any medical procedures during this time.

The second quarter is a time for bold, decisive action. Things will come easy, and there is a greater chance of a lucky break. This is a good time for weddings, especially if the moon will be in Libra, Cancer, or Taurus. Nevertheless, it is a good idea to put off any advertising activities and public speaking until closer to the full moon, if you can.

Full Moon

During the full moon, the Earth is located between the sun and the moon. During this time, the moon is round and fully illuminated. This takes place during days 14-16 of the lunar cycle.

During the full moon, many people feel more vigorous than usual. They are emotional, sociable, and actively seeking more contact, so this may be a good time for any celebrations.

However, be careful not to drink too much – you can relax to the point that you lose control, and the consequences of that can be very unpleasant. If you are able to stick to moderation, there is no better time for a party!

The full moon is also the best time for advertising, as not only will your campaign be widely seen, people will be apt to remember it.

The full moon is also a favorable time for dates, and during this time, people are at their most open, romantic, and willing to tell each other something important that might take their relationship to the next level of trust and understanding.

Moreover, during the full moon, people feel a surge of energy, which may lead to hyperactivity, restlessness, and insomnia.

It will be harder to keep your emotions in check. You might face conflicts with friends, disasters, and accidents. During the full moon, any surgeries are **not a good idea**, as the risk of complications and bleeding is on the rise. Plastic surgery is also a bad idea, as swelling and bruises might be much worse than in another lunar phase. At the same time, the full moon is a good time to get an accurate diagnosis.

During this time, try to limit your calories and liquid intake (especially if you deal with bloating and excess weight), as your body is absorbing both calories and liquids faster during the full moon, and it can be very difficult to get rid of the weight later on.

Waning Crescent Moon

The full moon is over, and a new phase is beginning – the waning moon. This is a quieter time, when all of the jobs you started earlier are being partly or entirely completed (it all depends on the speed and scale).

Surgery will turn out much better if it is performed during the waning moon. Your recovery will be faster, and the likelihood of complications is much lower. If you have any plans to lose weight, the waning moon is the best time to do that. This is also a good time for quitting bad habits, such as smoking or cursing.

The waning moon can also be divided into the third and fourth quarters.

Third quarter - this is a favorable period, and you are able to resolve a lot of problems without conflict. People are calming down and ready to listen and take in information, while still being active. However, this is not the best time to begin any major projects, especially if you are unsure if you will be able to complete them by the start of the new lunar month.

The third quarter is a good time to get married, especially if the moon is in Cancer, Taurus, or Libra.

Fourth quarter – This is the most passive period of the lunar cycle. You are not as strong as usual. Your energy is lagging. You will be tired until reaching a new beginning. The best thing you can do as the lunar cycle comes to an end is to get things in order, and avoid anything that might get in your way at work or in personal relationships. Examine your successes and failures.

Now, let's discuss the lunar days in greater detail. For centuries, people around the world have described the influence of lunar days, and modern astrologers only add to this work, as they compare old texts to modern life.

The 1st lunar day

The first lunar day is extremely important for the rest of the lunar month. This is a much-needed day to carefully plan your activities and lay the groundwork for the rest of the lunar month. Remember that the first lunar day is not a good day for major activities, but rather for sitting down and planning things.

Avoid conflicts on this day, unless you want them to overshadow the rest of the month. Try to see the positive side of things and imagine that the lunar month will bring you good things both at work and in love. The more vividly you can imagine this, the sooner your desires will come to fruition. Perhaps it would be a good idea to jot down plans that will bring you closer to achieving your dreams. This is the best time for both manifesting and making wishes!

This is also a favorable day when it comes to seeking a new job or starting an academic program.

It is fine to go out on a date on the first lunar day, but limit any sexual contact, as your energy levels are low, and you are likely to end up disappointed.

Getting married on the first lunar day is not recommended.

Avoid getting a haircut – there are many indications that cutting your hair on the first lunar day will have a negative effect on your health and life expectancy.

Under no circumstances should you undergo any major cosmetic procedures, including plastic surgery. Energy levels are low, your skin is dull and almost stagnant. The results will not live up to your expectations, and in the worst-case scenario, you will end up looking worse than before. It is common for cosmetic procedures performed on this day to be disappointing or even useless. Even the best surgeons are less capable.

Your good dreams on the first lunar day foretell happiness and joy. Bad ones usually do not come true.

The 2ⁿᵈ lunar day

This is considered a lucky day, and is symbolized by a cornucopia. It is not an exaggeration to say that the second lunar day is a favorable time for both work and love. It is a time for action, and a great period to work on yourself, look for a new job, start something new, or complete any financial transaction, whether a sale or purchase. This is also a great time for creative and scientific insights, and a good time for any meeting – whether political or romantic.

Any romantic dates or sexual encounters during the second lunar day are unlikely to disappoint. This is also a good day for weddings or taking a trip with someone special.

During the second lunar day, the moon is beginning its waxing phase, which is a good time for anything you might to do nourish and restore your skin. This is a great time for any cosmetic procedures aimed at preservation, though it is best to put off any plastic surgery until the waning moon. If that is not possible, then the second lunar day is acceptable, if not ideal, and you will not run into any complications.

Folklore tells us that this is not a good day for a haircut, as that may lead to arguments with a loved one.

This is the best time for exercise – your body is in good shape, and you are able to handle new exercise regimens. If the moon happens to be in Scorpio, though, be careful.

This is a good day for anything positive, but avoid any conflicts, discussions about the status of your relationship, or litigation.

Dreams of the second lunar day are usually not prophetic.

The 3rd lunar day

On this day, we are usually able to make out a thin sliver of the lunar crescent. It is a longstanding tradition to show money during the new month – it is believed that as the moon grows, so will your savings.

However, astrological systems around the world consider this an unlucky, unfavorable day. It is not a good idea to travel, begin any new business, or give into your bad mood.

You might run into many a lot of problems at work on this day, which will cause you a lot of anxiety. However, it is a good day to take a step back and identify and set about fixing any flaws and shortcomings. Remember that everything tends to look worse on this day than it actually is.

It is not the time to ask management for anything – you are likely to walk away disappointed, and end up unfairly reprimanded rather than receiving a promotion or raise. Instead, focus on areas of work that need to be smoothed over or studied further. It will be clear what problems you are facing, and you will easily be able to find a remedy.

Do not rush to criticize your loved ones – things may not be as they appear. "Measure twice and cut once" is your motto on this day.

This is not a good day to get married, as the couple is likely to have a turbulent, short-lived marriage.

You can schedule a cosmetic procedure for this day, but only if it is relatively minor. Plastic surgery should wait.

Do exercises as usual, without overdoing it or adding any new routines.

Dreams on this day do not mean anything.

The 4th lunar day

These are relatively neutral days, in that they are unlikely to bring anything bad, but they also will not bring you any windfalls. The fourth lunar day is symbolized by a tree of paradise, the tree of knowledge, and the choice between good and evil. Things ultimately depend on us and our final decisions.

This is a great day for anything money-related – signing contracts, agreements, or even taking on credit. There are also a lot of contradictions on this day – on one hand, we are likely to receive money, which is a good thing, but on the other, we will have to give some of it away, which is never particularly fun or pleasant. There is good reason to consider all of your opportunities and possibilities before acting.

It is not a good day to get married, as the wedding will not be as fun as you had hoped. However, the fourth lunar day is, in fact, a good day for sex and conceiving a healthy child.

Be careful on this day if you happen to engage in any physical exercise, as it is not a good idea to overeat or abuse alcohol. Take care of yourself. Any illnesses which began on this day may be extremely dangerous, if they are not dealt with immediately.

Cosmetic procedures are not contraindicated, as long as they are to preserve your appearance. Plastic surgery can be performed if you truly feel it is necessary.

However, avoid getting a haircut, as it is unlikely to grow back healthily, and will become brittle and dull. However, if the moon is in Leo, you can disregard this advice.

Dreams may turn out to be real.

The 5th lunar day

Traditionally, the fifth lunar day is one of the worst of the lunar month. It is symbolized by a unicorn. Unicorns need to be tamed, but only a virgin is capable of doing so. Many people will feel drained on this day, or frustrated with themselves, those around them, and life in general.

Try to avoid arguments- any conflicts are likely to drag out for a long time, and then you may be overcome with guilt. This advice is relevant for both work and love.

Sexual encounters may be pleasant, but this is not a good day to plan a wedding, as it is likely to lead to a marriage full of unpleasant incidents.

Do not start any new businesses, or ask those around you for favors- you may be misunderstood and rejected.

It is fine to engage in physical exercise, but if you overdo it on this day, you may injure yourself.

Your energy levels are low. Cosmetic procedures may not be effective, and avoid any plastic surgeries.

It is good if you dream something connected with the road, trips or with movement in general. A bad dream might be a sign of a health problem which should be addressed.

The 6th lunar day

The symbol of the sixth lunar day is a cloud and a crane. This is a philosophical combination that suggests that it is not worth rushing things on these days. This is a very positive, lucky day for both work and love. Creative work will be especially successful, as will any attempts at opening a new business in your field.

The sixth lunar day is a good time for resolving any financial matters. There is one limitation, however – do not give anyone a loan, as they may not pay it back. But you can certainly sponsor and support those who are more vulnerable than you.

This day is a good time to go on a trip, whether close to home or far away.

This is also a good day for dates, weddings, and marriage proposals. Remember that energy is more romantic than sexual, so it is better to give the gift of roses and a bottle of champagne than hot, passionate sex.

It is a good idea to get some exercise, but do not overdo things, though you will probably not want to, either.

Cosmetic procedures will be successful, and you can even have plastic surgery performed, so long as the moon is not in Scorpio.

It is still a good idea to avoid getting your hair cut, as you might "cut off" something good in addition to your hair.

It is better to not discuss dreams as they are usually true. Your dreams of this day can remind you of something that needs to be completed as soon as possible.

The 7th lunar day

This is also a favorable lunar day, and it is symbolized by a fighting cock, which is an Avestan deity. Avoid any aggression on this day, and instead work on yourself, spend time at home or in nature. Avoid discussing the status of your relationship with anyone, arguing, or wishing bad things on anyone. Everything will come back to haunt you, remember, silence is golden.

Business negotiations and contracts will be successful. You can find support, sponsors, and people ready to help you in both words and deeds.

Lighten up with your colleagues and subordinates. Pay attention not only to their shortcomings, but also to their skills. This is a good day for reconciliation and creating both political and romantic unions.

The seventh lunar day is good for traveling, no matter how near or far from home.

It is also a favorable time for love and marriage.

Exercise moderately, and any plastic surgeries will go very smoothly, as long as the moon is not in Scorpio.

Dreams of this day may become a reality.

The 8th lunar day

The symbol for this day is a Phoenix, which symbolizes eternal rebirth and renewal, because this day is a great time for changes in all areas of your life. Your energy is likely to be high, and you want to do something new and unusual. This is a good time to look for a new job or begin studying something. Any out-of-the-box thinking is welcome, along with shaking things up a bit in order to improve your life.

However, avoid any financial transactions, as you may incur losses.

Avoid aggression. You can share your opinion by presenting well-founded arguments and facts, instead.

The phoenix rises from the ashes, so this is a good time to be careful with electrical appliances and fire in general. The risk of housefires is high.

Avoid any major financial transactions on the eighth day, as you may end up facing a series of complications. You can pay people their salaries, as this is unlikely to be a large sum.

This is a good day for weddings, but only if you and your future spouse are restless, creative souls and hope to achieve personal development through your marriage.

Any cosmetic procedures and plastic surgeries will go well today, as they are related to rebirth and renewal. Surgeons may find that they are true artists on this day!

You can try to change your hairstyle and get a fashionable haircut on this day.

You can trust your dreams seen on this day.

The 9th lunar day

The ninth lunar day is not particularly auspicious, and is even referred to as "Satan's" day. You may be overcome with doubt, suspicions, even depression and conflicts.

Your self-esteem will suffer, so don't overdo things physically, and avoid overeating or abusing alcohol.

This is a negative day for any business deals, travel, or financial transactions.

This is a particularly bad day for any events, so keep your head down at work and avoid any new initiatives.

It is better to avoid getting married on "Satan's" day, as the marriage will not last very long. Avoid sex, as well, but you can take care of your partner, listen them, and support them however they need.

Any cosmetic procedures will not have a lasting effect, and avoid any plastic surgery. A haircut will not turn out as you hoped.

Dreams of this day are usually prophetic.

The 10th lunar day

This is one of the luckiest days of the lunar month. It is symbolized by a spring, mushroom, or phallus. This is a time for starting a new business, learning new things, and creating.

The 10th lunar day is particularly lucky for business. Networking and financial transactions will be a success and bring hope. This is an ideal time for changing jobs, shifting your business tactics, and other renewals.

This is a perfect time for people in creative fields and those working in science, who may come up with incredible ideas that will bring many successful returns.

This is a very successful day for building a family and proposing marriage. This is a good time for celebrations and communication, so plan parties, meet with friends, and plan a romantic date.

One of the symbols for this day is a phallus, so sexual encounters are likely to be particularly satisfying.

The 10th lunar day is the best time to begin repairs, buying furniture, and items for home improvement.

You can exercise vigorously, and cosmetic procedures and plastic surgery will be very effective.

Dreams of this day will not come true.

The 11th lunar day

This is one of the best lunar days, and seen as the pinnacle of the lunar cycle. People are likely to be energetic, enthusiastic, and ready to move forward toward their goals.

The 11th lunar day is very successful for any financial transactions or business deals and meetings.

You might actively make yourself known, approach management to discuss a promotion, or look for a new job. This is an auspicious time for advertising campaigns, performances, and holding meetings.

Any trips planned will be a great success, whether near or far from home.

Romantic relationships are improving, sex is harmonious, and very desired.

Weddings held on this day will be fun, and the marriage will be a source of joy and happiness.

Exercise is a great idea, and you might even beat your own personal record.

This is an ideal time for any cosmetic procedures, but any more serious plastic surgeries might lead to a lot of bruising and swelling.

A haircut will turn out as you had hoped, and you can experiment a bit with your appearance.

You can ignore dreams of this day – usually they do not mean anything.

The 12th lunar day

This day is symbolized by the Grail and a heart. As we move closer to the full moon, our emotions are at their most open. During this time, if you ask someone for something, your request will be heeded. This is a day of faith, goodness, and divine revelations.

For business and financial transactions, this is not the most promising day. However, if you help others on this day, your good deeds are sure to come back to you.

This is a day for reconciliation, so do not try to explain your relationships, as no one is at fault, and it is better to focus on yourself, anyway.

Avoid weddings and sex on this day, but if you want to do what your partner asks, there is no better time.

Many may feel less than confident and cheerful during this day, so take it easy when working out. Avoid overeating, stay hydrated, and avoid alcohol.

The 12th lunar day is not the best for getting married or having sex, but the stars would welcome affection and a kind word.

Avoid getting a haircut, or any plastic surgeries. This is a neutral day for minor cosmetic procedures.

Nearly all dreams will come true.

The 13th lunar day

This day is symbolized by Samsara, the wheel of fate, which is very erratic and capable of moving in any direction. This is why the 13th lunar day is full of contradictions. In Indian traditions, this day is compared to a snake eating its own tail. This is a day for paying off old debts and returning to unfinished business.

Avoid beginning any new business on this day. It is preferable to finish old tasks and proofread your work. Information you receive on this day may not be reliable and must be verified.

It is worth resolving financial problems very carefully, and avoid arguments and conflict.

Do not change jobs on this day or go to a new place for the first time. Do not sit at home alone, though, go see old friends, parents, or older family members.

Minor cosmetic procedures are welcome on this day, but avoid any plastic surgery, as you may experience major swelling and bruising. Avoid any haircuts, too.

As a rule, all dreams will come true.

The 14th lunar day

It's a full moon! The 14th lunar day is one of the happiest, and it is symbolized by the trumpet. Pay attention – you may run into new, much-needed information. Networking will be successful, and you can confidently sign agreements, meet with people, and attend fun gatherings or other leisure activities. This is one of the best days for advertising, performances, and concerts, and those working in creative professions should keep this in mind, as should those who work in politics. Do not sit in place on this day – you need to get out and see others, make new connections, and try to be visible.

This is one of the best days for communication with and making requests from management, as your initiatives will be noticed and welcome. You might talk about a promotion, raise, or something similarly related to professional growth.

Couples will see their relationship is moving along well on this day, and it is also a good day for getting married.

Any sex on this day will be vigorous and memorable for a long time. The full moon is the best time for conceiving a child.

Any cosmetic procedures will be effective, but avoid any major changes to your appearance, as there is a high likelihood of bleeding and bruising. A haircut will turn out well.

Your dreams of this day will be more or less doubtful.

The 15th lunar day

It's a full moon! This day is symbolized by a serpent of fire. This is the energy peak of the entire lunar cycle, and a lot will depend on where you are focusing your energy.

You might face a lot of temptations on this day, for example, you might tell someone else's secret or your own to others, and come to regret it for a long time. The stars suggest exercising restraint in both your words and actions, as the 15th day of the lunar cycle is a day of deception and weaknesses.

This is a very active time, and many people might take unnecessary risks. This is not the best day for signing any agreements or contracts. For any performances, concerts, or advertising, however, this is one of the best days of the month.

You can get married on the 15th day, but only if you know each other well and have carefully considered your partnership, without any hasty decisions. This is also a favorable day for a second marriage.

Your romantic relationship is looking wonderful – you are on cloud 9, writing poetry, and deeply convinced of how right your partner is for you – and they feel the same way. It is important that this does not suddenly lead to an abrupt disappointment.

Avoid getting any haircuts on the 15th day of the month, as you may end up with a headache.

Conservative cosmetic procedures and creams will be very effective, but avoid any injections or plastic surgery today. Bleeding, swelling, and bruising are all but guaranteed.

Dreams on the 15th day nearly always come true.

The 16th lunar day

This day is symbolized by a dove. The full moon is over, and the moon is now in its waning phase. Usually, after the turbulent days of the full moon, people feel a bit under the weather. They are not cheerful, and want to avoid excess worry and give themselves a chance to breathe.

Don't ignore your body's wishes, take it easy with physical activities, and take some time for yourself. You might spend time in nature, in the forest, or at a country home.

The 16th day of the lunar month is a time for moderation in all areas – your behavior, eating, and even in your clothes. If you overate during the full moon period, now is the time to diet a bit or at least avoid fatty foods and meat.

This is not a promising day for resolving any financial matters. Keep your documents in order and get ready for any future meetings, instead. If you help a loved one, your good deed will come back 100 times over.

Avoid getting married today, as well as sex.

Cosmetic procedures are likely to be a success, especially if they are related to cleansing your skin, but it is best to avoid any plastic surgery or injections. Your body is not ready to accept them. A haircut will turn out as you hoped.

Any dreams are likely to come true, but that also depends on a correct interpretation.

The 17th lunar day

This day is represented by a vine and bell. It is a happy day and both successful and fun-filled. It is also a good time for negotiations, concluding small business deals, shaking up staffing, and creativity. However, you should keep in mind that the 17th day is only favorable for minor business, and you should avoid starting any major events.

Avoid any major financial transactions on this day. Do not give anyone money as a loan or borrow anything yourself, either.

Any travel, whether for business or pleasure, is likely to be a success.

The 17th day is a great time to get married, and an ideal day for dates. Any sexual encounters will bring you happiness and joy.

Avoid getting your hair cut on this day, but cosmetic procedures and plastic surgery will be a success. Women will look better than usual.

Your dreams are likely to come true in three days.

The 18th lunar day

This day is represented by a mirror. It is a difficult, and generally unpromising day, too. Just as the mirror reflects our imperfections back to us, we need to remember that moderation and modesty are key.

The 18th day is not a favorable time for any business meetings or financial transactions. You can, however work on jobs you already began. It is, however, a positive day for those who work in research or the creative fields.

Your motto of the day is to keep a cool head when it comes to your opportunities and the opportunities of those around you. This is relevant for both work and romantic relationships. It is not a good time to criticize others – any conflicts or arguments may lead to lasting consequences, which you do not need.

Avoid getting married on this day, as well as sexual encounters, which are likely to be disappointing. It is a good time to take a trip together, which will only be good for your relationship.

Avoid getting your hair cut, though this is a relatively neutral day for a haircut, which might turn out well, and though it will not exceed your expectations, it will also not leave you upset. Avoid any plastic surgeries.

Dreams on this day will come true.

The 19th lunar day

This is a very difficult day and it is represented by a spider. The energy is complicated, if not outright dangerous. Don't panic or get depressed, though – this is a test of your strength, and if you are able to hold onto all you have achieved. This is relevant for both work and love. On the 19th day, you should avoid taking any trips.

The energy of the 19th lunar day is very unfavorable for beginning any major projects, and business in general. Work on what you started earlier, get your affairs in order, think over your ideas and emotions, and check to make sure that everything you have done hitherto is living up to your expectations. Do not carry out any financial transactions or take out any loans – do not loan anyone else money, either. Do not ask your managers for anything as they are unlikely to listen to what you have to say, and make judgments instead.

This is a day when you might face outright deception, so do not take any risks and ignore rumors. Do not work on anything related to real estate or legal matters.

This is a very hard time for people with an unbalanced psyche, as they may experience sudden exacerbations or even suicidal ideations.

This is a very unlucky day to get married. Sexual encounters might be disappointing and significantly worsen your relationship.

Avoid any haircuts or cosmetic procedures or surgeries.

Your dreams of this day will come true.

The 20th lunar day

This is also a difficult day, though less so than the 19th. It is represented by an eagle. This is a good time to work on your own development and spiritual growth, by speaking to a psychologist or astrologer.

Avoid pride, anger, arrogance, and envy.

The 20th lunar day is a good time for people who are active and decisive. They will be able to easily overcome any obstacles, flying over them just like an eagle. If you have to overcome your own fears, you will be able to do so – don't limit yourself, and you will see that there is nothing to be afraid of. It is a good day for any financial transactions, signing contracts, and reaching agreements, as well as networking.

The 20th lunar day is a favorable time for those who work in the creative fields, as they will be able to dream up the idea that will open up a whole host of new possibilities. Avoid conflicts – they may ruin your relationship with a lot of people, and it will not be easy to come back from that.

This is a lucky day for getting married, but only if you have been with your partner for several years, now. Sexual encounters will not be particularly joyful, but they also will not cause you any problems.

Avoid getting your hair cut, but you can certainly get it styled. The 20th lunar day is a good day for those who are looking to lose weight. You will be able to do so quickly, and it will be easy for you to follow a diet.

Cosmetic procedures will be a success, as will any plastic surgeries.

Pay attention to dreams of this day as they are likely to come true.

The 21st lunar day

This is one of the most successful days of the lunar month, and it is symbolized by a herd of horses – imagine energy, strength, speed, and bravery. Everything you think up will happen quickly, and you will be able to easily overcome obstacles. A mare is not only brave but also an honest animal, so you will only experience this luck if you remember that honesty is always the best policy.

This is also a favorable day for business. Reaching new agreements and signing contracts, or dealing with foreign partners – it is all likely to be a success. Any financial issues will be resolved successfully.

Those in the creative world will be able to show off their talent and be recognized for their work. Anyone involved in the performing arts can expect success, luck, and recognition. A galloping herd of horses moves quickly, so you might transition to a new job, move to a new apartment, or go on a business trip or travel with your better half.

The 21st lunar day is one of the best to get married or have a sexual encounter.

This is a great time for athletes, hunters, and anyone who likes adventurous activities.

But for criminals and thieves, this is not a lucky or happy day – they will quickly be brought to justice.

Any haircuts or cosmetic procedures are likely to be a huge success and bring both beauty and happiness. You will recover quickly after any surgeries, perhaps without any swelling or bruising at all.

Dreams tend to not be reliable.

The 22nd lunar day

This day will be strange and contradictory. It is symbolized by the elephant Ganesha. According to Indian mythology, Ganesha is the patron saint of hidden knowledge. so this is a favorable day for anyone who is trying to learn more about the world and ready to find the truth, though this is often seen as a hopeless endeavor. This is a day for philosophers and wisemen and women. However, it is an inauspicious day for business, and unlikely to lead to resolving financial issues, signing contracts, agreements, or beginning new projects. You can expect trouble at work.

For creative people, and new employees, this is a successful day.

This is a good day for apologies and reconciliation.

Avoid getting married, though you can feel free to engage in sexual encounters.

For haircuts and cosmetic procedures, this is a fantastic day. Surgeries will also turn out, as long as the moon is not in Scorpio.

Dreams will come true.

The 23rd lunar day

This is a challenging day represented by a crocodile, which is a very aggressive animal. This is a day of strong energy, but it is also adventurous and tough. Your main task is to focus your energy in the right direction. There may be accidents, arguments, conflicts, fights, and violence, which is why it is important to strive for balance and calm.

Keep a close eye on your surroundings – there may be traitors or people who do not wish you well, so be careful.

However, this is still a favorable day for business – many problems will be resolved successfully. You are able to sign contracts and receive credit successfully, as long as you remain active and decisive in what you do.

This is not a day for changing jobs or working on real estate transactions or legal proceedings. This is not a favorable day for traveling, no matter how near or far you plan on going.

This is not a promising day to get married – things may end in conflict, if not an all-out brawl.

Sexual relations are not off the table, as long as the couple trusts one another.

Haircuts or cosmetic procedures will not turn out as you had hoped, so avoid them.

Dreams during this lunar day usually mean something opposite of what awaits you, so you can disregard them.

The 24ᵗʰ lunar day

This is a neutral, calm day that is symbolized by a bear. It is favorable for forgiveness and reconciliation.

This is also a good day for learning new things, reading, self-development, and taking time to relax in nature.

This is a great day for any type of financial activity, conferences, academic meetings, and faraway travel.

The 24th lunar day is a good time for love and getting married, as any marriage will be strong and lasting.

Cosmetic procedures and plastic surgery will be a success, and you can expect a speedy recovery.

Avoid getting a haircut on this day, however, as your hair will likely thin and grow back slowly.

Dreams of this lunar day are usually connected with your personal life.

The 25th lunar day

This is still another quiet day, symbolized by a turtle.

Just like a turtle, this is not a day to rush, and it is best to sit down and take stock of your life. This is a good time for resolving any personal problems, as the moon's energy makes it possible for you to calm down and find the right path.

This is also not a bad day for business. It is believed that any business you begin on this day is sure to be a success. This is especially the case for trade and any monetary activities.

The 25th lunar day is not a good day to get married, especially if the couple is very young.

This is a neutral day for sexual encounters, as the moon is waning, energy is low, so the decision is yours.

Avoid any cosmetic procedures, except those for cleansing your skin. This is not a favorable day for haircuts or plastic surgery – unless the moon is in Libra or Leo.

You can have a prophetic dream on this day.

The 26th lunar day

The 26th lunar day is full of contradictions and complicated. It is represented by a toad.

It is not time to start or take on something new, as nothing good will come of it. Avoid any major purchases, as you will later come to see that your money was wasted. The best thing you can do on this day is stay at home and watch a good movie or read a good book.

Avoid traveling on this day, as it may not turn out well.

The 26th lunar day is a negative day for any business negotiations and starting new businesses. Do not complete any business deals or financial transactions. Your colleagues may be arguing, and your managers may be dissatisfied. But if you have decided to leave your job, there is no better time to do so.

This is not a good day to get married, as both partners' expectations may fall flat, and they will soon be disappointed.

The waning moon carries a negative charge, so avoid any haircuts and surgeries, though you can get cosmetic procedures if they are relatively minor.

Your dreams will come true.

The 27th lunar day

The 27th lunar day is one of the best days of the month, and it is represented by a ship. You can boldly start any new business, which is sure to be promising. This is a great day for students, teachers, and learning new things. Any information that comes to you on this day may be extremely valuable and useful to you.

The 27th day is good for communication and travel, whether near or far from home, and no matter whether it is for work or pleasure.

This is also a good day for any professional activities or financial transactions. If there are people around you who need help, you must support them, as your good deeds will come back 100-fold.

Romantic dates will go well, though any weddings should be quiet and subdued. This is a particularly good day for older couples or second marriages.

The waning moon means that hair will grow back very slowly, but in general, you can expect a haircut to turn out well. This is a great day for plastic surgery or cosmetic procedures, as the results will be pleasing, and you will have a speedy recovery, without any bruising or swelling, most of the time.

However, beware if the moon is in Scorpio on this day – that is not a good omen for any plastic surgery.

Do not pay any attention to dreams on this day.

The 28th lunar day

This is another favorable day in the waning moon cycle, and it is represented by a lotus. This is a day of wisdom and spiritual awakening. If possible, spend part of the day in nature. It is important to take stock of the last month and decide what you need to do during its two remaining days.

This is a good time for any career development, changing jobs, conducting business, decision-making, and signing agreements, as well as going on a trip. You might conclude any business deal, hold negotiations, work with money and securities.

This is also a good day for any repairs or improvements around your home or apartment.

Anyweddingstodayshouldbesubduedandmodest,andrestrictedtofamily members only. A loud, raucous wedding might not turn out very well.

Your hair will grow slowly, but any haircuts will turn out very elegant and stylish. Cosmetic procedures and surgeries are not contraindicated. You will recover quickly with little bruising and swelling.

Do not take any dreams too seriously.

The 29th lunar day

This is one of the most difficult days of the lunar month, and it is considered a Satanic day, unlucky for everyone and everything. It is symbolized by an octopus.

This is a dark day, and many will feel melancholy, depression, and a desire to simply be left alone. This is a day full of conflict and injuries, so be careful everywhere and with everyone. If you can, avoid any travel, and be particularly careful when handling any sharp objects. Do not engage in any business negotiations, sign any contracts, or take part in any networking.

Astrologers believe that anything you start on this day will completely fall apart. For once and for all, get rid of things that are impeding you from living your life. This is a good time to avoid people who you do find unpleasant.

This is also a time for fasting and limitations for everyone. Do not hold any celebrations, weddings, or have sexual relations – these events may not turn out as you hoped, and instead bring you nothing but suffering and strife.

Avoid getting a haircut, as well, as it will not make you look more beautiful and your hair will come back lifeless and dull. Cosmetic procedures can go ahead, but avoid any surgeries.

Dreams are likely to be true.

The 30th lunar day

There is not always a 30th lunar day, as some lunar months have only 29 days. This day is represented by a swan. The 30th lunar day is usually very short, and sometimes, it lasts less than an hour. This is a time for forgiveness and calm.

You might take stock of the last month, while also avoiding anything you do not need around you. Pay back loans, make donations, reconcile with those who recently offended you, and stop speaking to people who cause you suffering.

This is a good time for tying up loose ends, and many astrologers believe that it is also a good day to start new business.

However, avoid celebrations or weddings on this day. Spouses will either not live long, or they will quickly grow apart.

Do not get a haircut on this day, though cosmetic procedures are possible, as long as you avoid any surgeries.

Dreams promise happiness and should come true.

A Guide to Zodiac Compatibility

Often, when we meet a person, we get a feeling that they are good and we take an instant liking to them. Another person, however, gives us immediate feelings of distrust, fear and hostility. Is there an astrological reason why people say that 'the first impression is the most accurate'? How can we detect those who will bring us nothing but trouble and unhappiness?

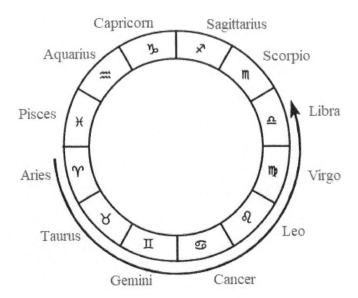

Without going too deeply into astrological subtleties unfamiliar to some readers, it is possible to determine the traits according to which friendship, love or business relationships will develop.

Let's begin with problematic relationships - our most difficult are with our **8th sign**. For example, for Aries the 8th sign is Scorpio, for Taurus it is Sagittarius and so on. Finding your 8th sign is easy; assume your own sign to be first (see above Figure) and then move eight signs counter clockwise around the Zodiac circle. This is also how the other signs (fourth, ninth and so on) that we mention are to be found.

Ancient astrologers variously referred to the 8th sign as the symbol of death, of destruction, of fated love or unfathomable attraction. In astrological terms, this pair is called 'master and slave' or 'boa constrictor and rabbit', with the role of 'master' or 'boa constrictor' being played by our 8th sign.

This relationship is especially difficult for politicians and business people.

We can take the example of a recent political confrontation in the USA. Hilary Clinton is a Scorpio while Donald Trump is a Gemini - her 8th sign. Even though many were certain that Clinton would be elected President, she lost.

To take another example, Hitler was a Taurus and his opponents – Stalin and Churchill - were both of his 8th sign, Sagittarius. The result of their confrontation is well known. Interestingly, the Russian Marshals who dealt crushing military blows to Hitler and so helped end the Third Reich - Konstantin Rokossovsky and Georgy Zhukov - were also Sagittarian, Hitler's 8th sign.

In another historical illustration, Lenin was also a Taurus. Stalin was of Lenin's 8th sign and was ultimately responsible for the downfall and possibly death of his one-time comrade-in-arms.

Business ties with those of our 8th sign are hazardous as they ultimately lead to stress and loss; both financial and moral. So, do not tangle with your 8th sign and never fight with it - your chances of winning are remote!

Such relationships are very interesting in terms of love and romance, however. We are magnetically attracted to our 8th sign and even though it may be very intense physically, it is very difficult for family life; 'Feeling bad when together, feeling worse when apart'.

As an example, let us take the famous lovers - George Sand who was Cancer and Alfred de Musset who was Sagittarius. Cancer is the 8th sign for Sagittarius, and the story of their crazy two-year love affair was the subject of much attention throughout France. Critics and writers were divided into 'Mussulist' and 'Sandist' camps; they debated fiercely about who was to blame for the sad ending to their love story - him or her. It's hard to imagine the energy needed to captivate the public for so long, but that energy was destructive for the couple. Passion raged in their hearts, but neither of them was able to comprehend their situation.

Georges Sand wrote to Musset, "*I don't love you anymore, and I will always adore you. I don't want you anymore, and I can't do without you. It seems that nothing but a heavenly lightning strike can heal me by destroying me. Good-bye! Stay or go, but don't say that I am not suffering. This is the only thing that can make me suffer even more, my love, my life, my blood! Go away, but kill me, leaving.*" Musset replied only in brief, but its power surpassed Sand's tirade, "*When you embraced me, I felt something that is still bothering me, making it impossible for me to approach another woman.*" These two people loved each other passionately and for two years lived together in a powder keg of passion, hatred and treachery.

When someone enters into a romantic liaison with their 8th sign, there will be no peace; indeed, these relationships are very attractive to those who enjoy the edgy, the borderline and, in the Dostoevsky style, the melodramatic. The first to lose interest in the relationship is, as a rule, the 8th sign.

If, by turn of fate, our child is born under our 8th sign, they will be very different from us and, in some ways, not live up to our expectations. It may be best to let them choose their own path.

In business and political relationships, the combination with our **12th sign** is also a complicated one.

We can take two political examples. Angela Merkel is a Cancer while Donald Trump is a Gemini - her 12th sign. This is why their relations are strained and complicated and we can even perhaps assume that the American president will achieve his political goals at her expense. Boris

Yeltsin (Aquarius) was the 12th sign to Mikhail Gorbachev (Pisces) and it was Yeltsin who managed to dethrone the champion of Perestroika.

Even ancient astrologers noticed that our relationships with our 12th signs can never develop evenly; it is one of the most curious and problematic combinations. They are our hidden enemies and they seem to be digging a hole for us; they ingratiate themselves with us, discover our innermost secrets. As a result, we become bewildered and make mistakes when we deal with them. Among the Roman emperors murdered by members of their entourage, there was an interesting pattern - all the murderers were the 12th sign of the murdered.

We can also see this pernicious effect in Russian history: the German princess Alexandra (Gemini) married the last Russian Tsar Nicholas II (Taurus) - he was her 12th sign and brought her a tragic death. The wicked genius Grigory Rasputin (Cancer) made friends with Tsarina Alexandra, who was his 12th sign, and was murdered as a result of their odd friendship. The weakness of Nicholas II was exposed, and his authority reduced after the death of the economic and social reformer Pyotr Stolypin, who was his 12th sign. Thus, we see a chain of people whose downfall was brought about by their 12th sign.

So, it makes sense to be cautious of your 12th sign, especially if you have business ties. Usually, these people know much more about us than we want them to and they will often reveal our secrets for personal gain if it suits them. However, the outset of these relationships is, as a rule, quite normal - sometimes the two people will be friends, but sooner or later one will betray the other one or divulge a secret; inadvertently or not.

In terms of romantic relationships, our 12th sign is gentle, they take care of us and are tender towards us. They know our weaknesses well but accept them with understanding. It is they who guide us, although sometimes almost imperceptibly. Sexual attraction is usually strong.

For example, Meghan Markle is a Leo, the 12th sign for Prince Harry, who is a Virgo. Despite Queen Elizabeth II being lukewarm about the match, Harry's love was so strong that they did marry.

If a child is our 12th sign, it later becomes clear that they know all our secrets, even those that they are not supposed to know. It is very difficult to control them as they do everything in their own way.

Relations with our **7th sign** are also interesting. They are like our opposite; they have something to learn from us while we, in turn, have something to learn from them. This combination, in business and personal relationships, can be very positive and stimulating provided that both partners are quite intelligent and have high moral standards but if not, constant misunderstandings and challenges follow. Marriage or co-operation with the 7th sign can only exist as the union of two fully-fledged individuals and in this case love, significant business achievements and social success are possible.

However, the combination can be not only interesting, but also quite complicated.

An example is Angelina Jolie, a Gemini, and Brad Pitt, a Sagittarius. This is a typical bond with a 7th sign - it's lively and interesting, but rather stressful. Although such a couple may quarrel and even part from time to time, never do they lose interest in each other.

This may be why this combination is more stable in middle-age when there is an understanding of the true nature of marriage and partnership. In global, political terms, this suggests a state of eternal tension - a cold war - for example between Yeltsin (Aquarius) and Bill Clinton (Leo).

Relations with our **9th sign** are very good; they are our teacher and advisor - one who reveals things we are unaware of and our relationships with them very often involve travel or re-location. The combination can lead to spiritual growth and can be beneficial in terms of business.

Although, for example, Trump and Putin are political opponents, they can come to an understanding and even feel a certain sympathy for each other because Putin is a Libra while Trump is a Gemini, his 9th sign.

This union is also quite harmonious for conjugal and romantic relationships.

We treat our **3rd sign** somewhat condescendingly. They are like our younger siblings; we teach them and expect them to listen attentively. Our younger brothers and sisters are more often than not born under this sign. In terms of personal and sexual relationships, the union is not very inspiring and can end quickly, although this is not always the case. In terms of business, it is fairly average as it often connects partners from different cities or countries.

We treat our **5th sign** as a child and we must take care of them accordingly. The combination is not very good for business, however, since our 5th sign triumphs over us in terms of connections and finances, and thereby gives us very little in return save for love or sympathy. However, they are very good for family and romantic relationships, especially if the 5th sign is female. If a child is born as a 5th sign to their parents, their relationship will be a mutually smooth, loving and understanding one that lasts a lifetime.

Our **10th sign** is a born leader. Depending on the spiritual level of those involved, both pleasant and tense relations are possible; the relationship is often mutually beneficial in the good times but mutually disruptive in the bad times. In family relations, our 10th sign always tries to lead and will do so according to their intelligence and upbringing.

Our **4th sign** protects our home and can act as a sponsor to strengthen our financial or moral positions. Their advice should be heeded in all cases as it can be very effective, albeit very unobtrusive. If a woman takes this role, the relationship can be long and romantic, since all the spouse's wishes are usually met one way or another. Sometimes, such couples achieve great social success; for instance, Hilary Clinton, a Scorpio is the 4th sign to Bill Clinton, a Leo. On the other hand, if the husband is the 4th sign for his wife, he tends to be henpecked. There is often a strong sexual attraction. Our 4th sign can improve our living conditions and care for us in a parental way. If a child is our 4th sign, they are close to us and support us affectionately.

Relations with our **11th sign** are often either friendly or patronizing; we treat them reverently, while they treat us with friendly condescension. Sometimes, these relationships develop in an 'older brother' or 'high-ranking friend' sense; indeed, older brothers and sisters are often our 11th sign. In terms of personal and sexual relationships, our 11th sign is always inclined to enslave us. This tendency is most clearly manifested in such alliances as Capricorn and Pisces or Leo and Libra. A child who is the 11th sign to their parents will achieve greater success than their parents, but this will only make the parents proud.

Our **2nd sign** should bring us financial or other benefits; we receive a lot from them in both our business and our family life. In married couples, the 2nd sign usually looks after the financial situation for the benefit of the family. Sexual attraction is strong.

Our **6th sign** is our 'slave'; we always benefit from working with them and it's very difficult for them to escape our influence. In the event of hostility, especially if they have provoked the conflict, they receive a powerful retaliatory strike. In personal relations, we can almost destroy them by making them dance to our tune. For example, if a husband doesn't allow his wife to work or there are other adverse family circumstances, she gradually becomes lost as an individual despite being surrounded by care. This is the best-case scenario; worse outcomes are possible. Our 6th sign has a strong sexual attraction to us because we are the fatal 8th sign for them; we cool down quickly, however, and often make all kinds of demands. If the relationship with our 6th sign is a long one, there is a danger that routine, boredom and stagnation will ultimately destroy the relationship. A child born under our 6th sign needs particularly careful handling as they can feel fear or embarrassment when communicating with us. Their health often needs increased attention and we should also remember that they are very different from us emotionally.

Finally, we turn to relations with **our own sign**. Scorpio with Scorpio and Cancer with Cancer get along well, but in most other cases, however, our own sign is of little interest to us as it has a similar energy. Sometimes, this relationship can develop as a rivalry, either in business or in love.

There is another interesting detail - we are often attracted to one particular sign. For example, a man's wife and mistress often have the same sign. If there is confrontation between the two, the stronger character displaces the weaker one. As an example, Prince Charles is a Scorpio, while both Princess Diana and Camilla Parker Bowles were born under the sign of Cancer. Camilla was the more assertive and became dominant.

Of course, in order to draw any definitive conclusions, we need an individually prepared horoscope, but the above always, one way or another, manifests itself.

Love Description of Zodiac Signs

We know that human sexual behavior has been studied at length. Entire libraries have been written about it, with the aim of helping us understand ourselves and our partners. But is that even possible? It may not be; no matter how smart we are, when it comes to love and sex, there is always an infinite amount to learn. But we have to strive for perfection, and astrology, with its millennia of research, twelve astrological types, and twelve zodiac signs, may hold the key. Below, you will find a brief and accurate description of each zodiac sign's characteristics in love, for both men and women.

Men

ARIES

Aries men are not particularly deep or wise, but they make up for it in sincerity and loyalty. They are active, even aggressive lovers, but a hopeless romantic may be lurking just below the surface. Aries are often monogamous and chivalrous men, for whom there is only one woman (of course, in her absence, they can sleep around with no remorse). If the object of your affection is an Aries, be sure to give him a lot of sex, and remember that for an Aries, when it comes to sex, anything goes. Aries cannot stand women who are negative or disheveled. They need someone energetic, lively, and to feel exciting feelings of romance.

The best partner for an Aries is Cancer, Sagittarius, or Leo. Aquarius can also be a good match, but the relationship will be rather friendly in nature. Partnering with a Scorpio or Taurus will be difficult, but they can be stimulating lovers for an Aries. Virgos are good business contacts, but a poor match as lovers or spouses.

TAURUS

A typical Taurean man is warm, friendly, gentle, and passionate, even if he doesn't always show it. He is utterly captivated by the beauty of the female body, and can find inspiration in any woman. A Taurus has such excess physical and sexual prowess, that to him, sex is a way to relax and calm down. He is the most passionate and emotional lover of the Zodiac, but he expects his partner to take the initiative, and if she doesn't, he will easily find someone else. Taureans rarely divorce, and are true to the end – if not sexually, at least spiritually. They are secretive, keep their cards close, and may have secret lovers. If a Taurus does not feel a deep emotional connection with someone, he won't be shy to ask her friends for their number. He prefers a voluptuous figure over an athletic or skinny woman.

The best partners for a Taurus are Cancer, Virgo, Pisces, or Scorpio. Sagittarius can show a Taurus real delights in both body and spirit, but they are unlikely to make it down the aisle. They can have an interesting relationship with an Aquarius – these signs are very different, but sometimes can spend their lives together. They might initially feel attracted to an Aries, before rejecting her.

GEMINI

The typical Gemini man is easygoing and polite. He is calm, collected, and analytical. For a Gemini, passion is closely linked to intellect, to the point that they will try to find an explanation for their actions before carrying them out. But passion cannot be explained, which scares a Gemini, and they begin jumping from one extreme to the other. This is why you will find more bigamists among Geminis than any other sign of the Zodiac. Sometimes, Gemini men even have two families, or divorce and marry several times throughout the course of their lives. This may be because they simply can't let new and interesting experiences pass them by. A Gemini's wife or lover needs to be smart, quick, and always looking ahead. If she isn't, he will find a new object for his affection.

Aquarians, Libras, and Aries make good partners for a Gemini. A Sagittarius can be fascinating for him, but they will not marry before he reaches middle age, as both partners will be fickle while they are younger. A Gemini and Scorpio are likely to be a difficult match, and the Gemini will try to wriggle out of the Scorpio's tight embrace. A Taurus will be an exciting sex partner, but their partnership won't be for long, and the Taurus is often at fault.

CANCER

Cancers tend to be deep, emotional individuals, who are both sensitive and highly sexual. Their charm is almost mystical, and they know how to use it. Cancers may be the most promiscuous sign of the Zodiac, and open to absolutely anything in bed. Younger Cancers look for women who are more mature, as they are skilled lovers. As they age, they look for someone young enough to be their own daughter, and delight in taking on the role of a teacher. Cancers are devoted to building a family and an inviting home, but once they achieve that goal, they are likely to have a wandering eye. They will not seek moral justification, as they sincerely believe it is simply something everyone does. Their charm works in such a way that women are deeply convinced they are the most important love in a Cancer's life, and that circumstances are the only thing preventing them from being together. Remember that a Cancer man is a master manipulator, and will not be yours unless he is sure you have throngs of admirers. He loves feminine curves, and is turned on by exquisite fragrances. Cancers don't end things with old lovers, and often go back for a visit after a breakup. Another type of Cancer is rarer – a faithful friend, and up for anything in order to provide for his wife and children. He is patriotic and a responsible worker.

Scorpios, Pisces, and other Cancers are a good match. A Taurus can make for a lasting relationship, as both signs place great value on family and are able to get along with one another. A Sagittarius will result in fights and blowouts from the very beginning, followed by conflicts and breakups. The Sagittarius will suffer the most. Marriage to an Aries isn't off the table, but it won't last very long.

LEO

A typical Leo is handsome, proud, and vain, with a need to be the center of attention at all times. They often pretend to be virtuous, until they are able to actually master it. They crave flattery, and prefer women who comply and cater to them. Leos demand unconditional obedience, and constant approval. When a Leo is in love, he is fairly sexual, and capable of being devoted and faithful. Cheap love affairs are not his thing, and Leos are highly aware of how expensive it is to divorce. They make excellent fathers. A Leo's partner needs to look polished and well-dressed, and he will not tolerate either frumpiness or nerds.

Aries, Sagittarius, and Gemini make for good matches. Leos are often very beguiling to Libras; this is the most infamous astrological "master-slave" pairing. Leos are also inexplicably drawn to Pisces – this is the only sign capable of taming them. A Leo and Virgo will face a host of problems sooner or later, and they might be material in nature. The Virgo will attempt to conquer him, and if she does, a breakup is inevitable.

VIRGO

Virgo is a highly intellectual sign, who likes to take a step back and spend his time studying the big picture. But love inherently does not lend itself to analysis, and this can leave Virgos feeling perplexed. While Virgo is taking his time, studying the object of his affection, someone else will swoop in and take her away, leaving him bitterly disappointed. Perhaps for that reason, Virgos tend to marry late, but once they are married, they remain true, and hardly ever initiate divorce. In bed, they are modest and reserved, as they see sex as some sort of quirk of nature, designed solely for procreation. Most Virgos have a gifted sense of taste, hearing, and smell. They cannot tolerate pungent odors and can be squeamish; they believe their partners should always take pains to be very clean. Virgos usually hate over-the-top expressions of love, and are immune to sex as a mean s of control. Many Virgos are stingy and more appropriate as husbands than lovers. Male Virgos tend to be monogamous, though if they are unhappy or disappointed with their partner, they may begin to look for comfort elsewhere and often give in to drunkenness.

Taurus, Capricorn, and Scorpio make the best partners for a Virgo. They may feel inexplicable attraction for Aquarians. They will form friendships with Aries, but rarely will this couple make it down the aisle. With Leos, be careful – this sign is best as a lover, not a spouse.

LIBRA

Libra is a very complex, wishy-washy sign. They are constantly seeking perfection, which often leaves them in discord with the reality around them. Libra men are elegant and refined, and expect no less from their partner. Many Libras treat their partners like a beautiful work of art, and have trouble holding onto the object of their affection. They view love itself as a very abstract concept, and can get tired of the physical aspect of their relationship. They are much more drawn to intrigue and the chase- dreams, candlelit evenings, and other symbols of romance. A high percentage of Libra men are gay, and they view sex with other men as the more elite option. Even when Libras are unhappy in their marriages, they never divorce willingly. Their wives might leave them, however, or they might be taken away by a more decisive partner.

Aquarius and Gemini make the best matches for Libras. Libra can also easily control an independent Sagittarius, and can easily fall under the influence of a powerful and determined Leo, before putting all his strength and effort into breaking free. Relationships with Scorpios are difficult; they may become lovers, but will rarely marry.

SCORPIO

Though it is common to perceive Scorpios as incredibly sexual, they are, in fact, very unassuming, and never brag about their exploits. They will, however, be faithful and devoted to the right woman. The Scorpio man is taciturn, and you can't expect any tender words from him, but he will defend those he loves to the very end. Despite his outward control, Scorpio is very emotional; he needs and craves love, and is willing to fight for it. Scorpios are incredible lovers, and rather than leaving them tired, sex leaves them feeling energized. They are always sexy, even if they aren't particularly handsome. They are unconcerned with the ceremony of wooing you, and more focused on the act of love itself.

Expressive Cancers and gentle, amenable Pisces make the best partners. A Scorpio might also fall under the spell of a Virgo, who is adept at taking the lead. Sparks might fly between two Scorpios, or with a Taurus, who is perfect for a Scorpio in bed. Relationships with Libras, Sagittarians, and Aries are difficult.

SAGITTARIUS

Sagittarian men are lucky, curious, and gregarious. Younger Sagittarians are romantic, passionate, and burning with desire to experience every type of love. Sagittarius is a very idealistic sign, and in that search for perfection, they tend to flit from one partner to another, eventually forgetting what they were even looking for in the first place. A negative Sagittarius might have two or three relationships going on at once, assigning each partner a different day of the week. On the other hand, a positive Sagittarius will channel his powerful sexual energy into creativity, and take his career to new heights. Generally speaking, after multiple relationships and divorces, the Sagittarian man will conclude that his ideal marriage is one where his partner is willing to look the other way.

Aries and Leo make the best matches for a Sagittarius. He might fall under the spell of a Cancer, but would not be happy being married to her. Gemini can be very intriguing, but will only make for a happy marriage after middle age, when both partners are older and wiser. Younger Sagittarians often marry Aquarian women, but things quickly fall apart. Scorpios can make for an interesting relationship, but if the Sagittarius fails to comply, divorce is inevitable.

CAPRICORN

Practical, reserved Capricorn is one of the least sexual signs of the Zodiac. He views sex as an idle way to pass the time, and something he can live without, until he wants to start a family. He tends to marry late, and almost never divorces. Young Capricorns are prone to suppressing their sexual desires, and only discover them later in life, when they have already achieved everything a real man needs – a career and money. We'll be frank – Capricorn is not the best lover, but he can compensate by being caring, attentive, and showering you with valuable gifts. Ever cautious, Capricorn loves to schedule his sexual relationships, and this is something partners will just have to accept. Women should understand that Capricorn needs some help relaxing – perhaps with alcohol. They prefer inconspicuous, unassuming women, and run away from a fashion plate.

The best partners for a Capricorn are Virgo, Taurus, or Scorpio. Cancers might catch his attention, and if they marry, it is likely to be for life. Capricorn is able to easily dominate Pisces, and Pisces-Capricorn is a well-known "slave and master" combination. Relationships with Leos tend to be erratic, and they are unlikely to wed. Aries might make for a cozy family at first, but things will cool off quickly, and often, the marriage only lasts as long as Capricorn is unwilling to make a change in his life.

AQUARIUS

Aquarian men are mercurial, and often come off as peculiar, unusual, or aloof, and detached. Aquarians are turned on by anything novel or strange, and they are constantly looking for new and interesting people. They are stimulated by having a variety of sexual partners, but they consider this to simply be normal life, rather than sexually immoral. Aquarians are unique – they are more abstract than realistic, and can be cold and incomprehensible, even in close relationships. Once an Aquarius gets married, he will try to remain within the realm of decency, but often fails. An Aquarian's partners need uncommon patience, as nothing they do can restrain him. Occasionally, one might encounter another kind of Aquarius – a responsible, hard worker, and exemplary family man.

The best matches for an Aquarius are female fellow Aquarians, Libras, and Sagittarians. When Aquarius seeks out yet another affair, he is not choosy, and will be happy with anyone.

PISCES

Pisces is the most eccentric sign of the Zodiac. This is reflected in his romantic tendencies and sex life. Pisces men become very dependent on those with whom they have a close relationship. Paradoxically, they are simultaneously crafty and childlike when it comes to playing games, and they are easily deceived. As a double bodied sign, Pisces rarely marry just once, as they are very sexual, easily fall in love, and are constantly seeking their ideal. Pisces are very warm people, who love to take care of others and are inclined toward "slave-master" relationships, in which they are the submissive partner. But after catering to so many lovers, Pisces will remain elusive. They are impossible to figure out ahead of time – today, they might be declaring their love for you, but tomorrow, they may disappear – possibly forever! To a Pisces, love is a fantasy, illusion, and dream, and they might spend their whole lives in pursuit of it. Pisces who are unhappy in love are vulnerable to alcoholism or drug addiction.

Cancer and Scorpio make the best partners for a Pisces. He is also easily dominated by Capricorn and Libra, but in turn will conquer even a queen-like Leo. Often, they are fascinated by Geminis – if they marry, it will last a long time, but likely not forever. Relationships with Aries and Sagittarians are erratic, though initially, things can seem almost perfect.

Women

ARIES

Aries women are leaders. They are decisive, bold, and very protective. An Aries can take initiative and is not afraid to make the first move. Her ideal man is strong, and someone she can admire. But remember, at the slightest whiff of weakness, she will knock him off his pedestal. She does not like dull, whiny men, and thinks that there is always a way out of any situation. If she loves someone, she will be faithful. Aries women are too honest to try leading a double life. They are possessive, jealous, and not only will they not forgive those who are unfaithful, their revenge may be brutal; they know no limits. If you can handle an Aries, don't try to put her in a cage; it is best to give her a long leash. Periodically give her some space – then she will seek you out herself. She is sexual, and believe that anything goes in bed.

Her best partners are a Sagittarius or Leo. A Libra can make a good match after middle age, once both partners have grown wiser and settled down a bit. Gemini and Aquarius are only good partners during the initial phase, when everything is still new, but soon enough, they will lose interest in each other. Scorpios are good matches in bed, but only suitable as lovers.

TAURUS

Taurean women possess qualities that men often dream about, but rarely find in the flesh – they are soft, charming, practical, and reliable – they are very caring and will support their partner in every way. A Taurus is highly sexual, affectionate, and can show a man how to take pleasure to new heights. She is also strong and intense. If she is in love, she will be faithful. But when love fades away, she might find someone else on the side, though she will still fight to save her marriage, particularly if her husband earns good money. A Taurus will not tolerate a man who is disheveled or disorganized, and anyone dating her needs to always be on his toes. She will expect gifts, and likes being taken to expensive restaurants, concerts, and other events. If you argue, try to make the first peace offering, because a Taurus finds it very hard to do so – she might withdraw and ruminate for a long time. Never air your dirty laundry; solve all your problems one-on-one.

Scorpio, Virgo, Capricorn, and Cancer make the best matches. A relationship with an Aries or Sagittarius would be difficult. There is little attraction between a Taurus and a Leo, and initially Libras can make for a good partner in bed, but things will quickly cool off and fall apart. A Taurus and Aquarius make an interesting match – despite the difference in signs, their relationships are often lasting, and almost lifelong.

GEMINI

Gemini women are social butterflies, outgoing, and they easily make friends, and then break off the friendship, if people do not hold their interest. A Gemini falls in love hard, is very creative, and often fantasizes about the object of her affection. She is uninterested in sex without any attachment, loves to flirt, and, for the most part, is not particularly affectionate. She dreams of a partner who is her friend, lover, and a romantic, all at once. A Gemini has no use for a man who brings nothing to the table intellectually. That is a tall order, so Geminis often divorce and marry several times. Others simply marry later in life. Once you have begun a life together, do not try to keep her inside – she needs to travel, explore, socialize, attend events and go to the theater. She cannot tolerate possessive men, so avoid giving her the third degree, and remember that despite her flirtatious and social nature, she is, in fact, faithful – as long as you keep her interested and she is in love. Astrologists believe that Geminis do not know what they need until age 29 or 30, so it is best to hold off on marriage until then.

Leo and Libra make the best matches. A relationship with a Cancer is likely, though complex, and depends solely on the Cancer's affection. A Gemini and Sagittarius can have an interesting, dynamic relationship, but these are two restless signs, which might only manage to get together after ages 40-45, once they have had enough thrills out of life and learned to be patient. Relationships with a Capricorn are very difficult, and almost never happen. The honeymoon stage can be wonderful with a Scorpio, but each partner will eventually go their own way, before ending things. A Gemini and Pisces union can also be very interesting – they are drawn to each other, and can have a wonderful relationship, but after a while, the cracks start to show and things will fall apart. An Aquarius is also not a bad match, but they will have little sexual chemistry.

CANCER

Cancers can be divided into two opposing groups. The first includes a sweet and gentle creature who is willing to dedicate her life to her husband and children. She is endlessly devoted to her husband, especially if he makes a decent living and remains faithful. She views all men as potential husbands, which means it is dangerous to strike up a relationship with her if your intentions are not serious; she can be anxious and clingy, sensitive and prone to crying. It is better to break things to her gently, rather than directly spitting out the cold, hard truth. She wants a man who can be a provider, though she often earns well herself. She puts money away for a rainy day, and knows how to be thrifty, for the sake of others around her, rather than only for herself. She is an excellent cook and capable of building an inviting home for her loved ones. She is enthusiastic in bed, a wonderful wife, and a caring mother.

The second type of Cancer is neurotic, and capable of creating a living hell for those around her. She believes that the world is her enemy, and manages to constantly find new intrigue and machinations.

Another Cancer, Virgo, Taurus, Scorpio, and Pisces make the best matches. A Cancer can often fall in love with a Gemini, but eventually, things will grow complicated, as she will be exhausted by a Gemini's constant mood swings and cheating. A Cancer and Sagittarius will initially have passionate sex, but things will quickly cool off. A relationship with a Capricorn is a real possibility, but only later in life, as while they are young, they are likely to fight and argue constantly. Cancer can also have a relationship with an Aries, but this will not be easy.

LEO

Leos are usually beautiful or charming, and outwardly sexual. And yet, appearances can be deceiving – they are not actually that interested in sex. Leo women want to be the center of attention and men running after them boosts their self-esteem, but they are more interested in their career, creating something new, and success than sex. They often have high-powered careers and are proud of their own achievements. Their partners need to be strong; if a Leo feels a man is weak, she can carry him herself for a while- before leaving him. It is difficult for her to find a partner for life, as chivalrous knights are a dying breed, and she is not willing to compromise. If you are interested in a Leo, take the initiative, admire her, and remember that even a queen is still a woman. Timid men or tightwads need not apply. Leos like to help others, but they don't need a walking disaster in their life. If they are married and in love, they are usually faithful, and petty gossip isn't their thing. Leo women make excellent mothers, and are ready to give their lives to their children. Their negative traits include vanity and a willingness to lie, in order to make themselves look better.

Sagittarius, Aries, and Libra make the best matches. Leos can also have an interesting relationship with a Virgo, though both partners will weaken each other. Life with a Taurus will lead to endless arguments – both signs are very stubborn, and unwilling to give in. Leos and Pisces are another difficult pair, as she will have to learn to be submissive if she wants to keep him around. A relationship with a Capricorn will work if there is a common denominator, but they will have little sexual chemistry. Life with a Scorpio will be turbulent to say the least, and they will usually break up later in life.

VIRGO

Virgo women are practical, clever, and often duplicitous. Marrying one isn't for everyone. She is a neat freak to the point of annoying those around her. She is also an excellent cook, and strives to ensure her children receive the very best by teaching them everything, and preparing them for a bright future. She is also thrifty – she won't throw money around, and, in fact, won't even give it to her husband. She has no time for rude, macho strongmen, and is suspicious of spendthrifts. She will not be offended if you take her to a cozy and modest café rather than an elegant restaurant. Virgos are masters of intrigue, and manage to outperform every other sign of the Zodiac in this regard. Virgos love to criticize everyone and everything; to listen to them, the entire world is simply a disaster and wrong, and only she is the exception to this rule. Virgos are not believed to be particularly sexual, but there are different variations when it comes to this. Rarely, one finds an open-minded Virgo willing to try anything, and who does it all on a grand scale – but she is rather the exception to this general rule.

The best matches for a Virgo are Cancer, Taurus, and Capricorn. She also can get along well with a Scorpio, but will find conflict with Sagittarius. A Pisces will strike her interest, but they will rarely make it down the aisle. She is often attracted to an Aquarius, but they would drive each other up the wall were they to actually marry. An Aries forces Virgo to see another side of life, but here, she will have to learn to conform and adapt.

LIBRA

Female Libras tend to be beautiful, glamorous, or very charming. They are practical, tactical, rational, though they are adept at hiding these qualities behind their romantic and elegant appearance. Libras are drawn to marriage, and are good at imagining the kind of partner they need. They seek out strong, well-off men and are often more interested in someone's social status and bank account than feelings. The object of their affection needs to be dashing, and have a good reputation in society. Libras love expensive things, jewelry, and finery. If they are feeling down, a beautiful gift will instantly cheer them up. They will not tolerate scandal or conflict, and will spend all their energy trying to keep the peace, or at least the appearance thereof. They do not like to air their dirty laundry, and will only divorce in extreme circumstances. They are always convinced they are right and react to any objections as though they have been insulted. Most Libras are not particularly sexual, except those with Venus or the Moon in Scorpio.

Leos, Geminis, and Aquarians make good matches. Libra women are highly attracted to Aries men - this is a real case of opposites attract. They can get along with a Sagittarius, though he will find that Libras are too proper and calm. Capricorn, Pisces, and Cancer are all difficult matches. Things will begin tumultuously with a Taurus, before each partner goes his or her own way.

SCORPIO

Scorpio women may appear outwardly restrained, but there is much more bubbling below the surface. They are ambitious with high self-esteem, but often wear a mask of unpretentiousness. They are the true power behind the scenes, the one who holds the family together, but never talk about it. Scorpios are strong-willed, resilient, and natural survivors. Often, Scorpios are brutally honest, and expect the same out of those around them. They do not like having to conform, and attempt to get others to adapt to them, as they honestly believe everyone will be better off that way. They are incredibly intuitive, and not easily deceived. They have an excellent memory, and can quickly figure out which of your buttons to push. They are passionate in bed, and their temperament will not diminish with age. When she is sexually frustrated, a Scorpio will throw all of her energy into her career or her loved ones. She is proud, categorical, and "if you don't do it right, don't do it at all" is her motto. Scorpio cannot be fooled, and she will not forgive any cheating. Will she cheat herself? Yes! But it will not break up her family, and she will attempt to keep it a secret. Scorpios are usually attractive to men, even if they are not particularly beautiful. They keep a low profile, though they always figure out their partner, and give them some invisible sign. There is also another, selfish type of Scorpio, who will use others for as long as they need them, before unceremoniously casting them aside.

Taurus is a good match; they will have excellent sexual chemistry and understand each other. Scorpio and Gemini are drawn to each other, but are unlikely to stay together long enough to actually get married. Cancer can be a good partner as well, but Cancers are possessive, while Scorpios do not like others meddling in their affairs, though they can later resolve their arguments in bed. Scorpio and Leo are often found together, but their relationship can also be very complicated. Leos are animated and chipper, while Scorpios, who are much deeper and more stubborn, see Leos as not particularly serious or reliable. One good example of this is Bill (a Leo) and Hillary (a Scorpio) Clinton. Virgo can also make a good partner, but when Scorpio seemingly lacks emotions, he will look for them elsewhere. Relationships with Lira are strange and very rare. Scorpio sees Libra as too insecure, and Libra does not appreciate Scorpio's rigidity. Two Scorpios together make an excellent marriage! Sagittarius and Scorpio are unlikely to get together, as she will think he is shallow and rude. If they do manage to get married, Scorpio's drive and persistence is the only thing that will make the marriage last. Capricorn is also not a bad match, and while Scorpio finds Aquarius attractive, they will rarely get married, as they are simply speaking different languages! Things are alright with a Pisces, as both signs are emotional, and Pisces can let Scorpio take the lead when necessary.

SAGITTARIUS

Sagittarius women are usually charming, bubbly, energetic, and have the gift of gab. They are kind, sincere, and love people. They are also straightforward, fair, and very ambitious, occasionally to the point of irritating those around them. But telling them something is easier than not telling them, and they often manage to win over their enemies. Sagittarius tends to have excellent intuition, and she loves to both learn and teach others. She is a natural leader, and loves taking charge at work and at home. Many Sagittarian women have itchy feet, and prefer all kinds of travel to sitting at home. They are not particularly good housewives – to be frank, cooking and cleaning is simply not for them. Their loved ones must learn to adapt to them, but Sagittarians themselves hate any pressure. They are not easy for men to handle, as Sagittarians want to be in charge. Sagittarius falls in love easily, is very sexual and temperamental, and may marry multiple times. Despite outward appearances, Sagittarius is a very lonely sign. Even after she is married with children, she may continue living as if she were alone; you might say she marches to the beat of her own drum. Younger

Sagittarians can be reckless, but as they mature, they can be drawn to religion, philosophy, and the occult.

Aries and Leo make the best matches, as Sagittarius is able to bend to Leo's ways, or at least pretend to. Sagittarians often end up with Aquarians, but their marriages do not tend to be for the long haul. They are attracted to Geminis, but are unlikely to marry one until middle age, when both signs have settled down. Sagittarius and Cancer have incredible sexual chemistry, but an actual relationship between them would be tumultuous and difficult. Capricorn can make a good partner- as long as they are able to respect each other's quirks. Sagittarius rarely ends up with a Virgo, and while she may often meet Pisces, things are unlikely to go very far.

CAPRICORN

Capricorn women are conscientious, reliable, organized, and hard-working. Many believe that life means nothing but work, and live accordingly. They are practical, and not particularly drawn to parties or loud groups of people. But if someone useful will be there, they are sure to make an appearance. Capricorn women are stingy, but not as much as their male counterparts. They are critical of others, but think highly of themselves. Generally, they take a difficult path in life, but thanks to their dedication, perseverance, and willingness to push their own limits, they are able to forge their own path, and by 45 or 50, they can provide themselves with anything they could want. Capricorn women have the peculiarity of looking older than their peers when they are young, and younger than everyone else once they have matured. They are not particularly sexual, and tend to be faithful partners. They rarely divorce, and even will fight until the end, even for a failed marriage. Many Capricorns have a pessimistic outlook of life, and have a tendency to be depressed. They are rarely at the center of any social circle, but are excellent organizers. They have a very rigid view of life and love, and are not interested in a fling, as marriage is the end goal. As a wife, Capricorn is simultaneously difficult and reliable. She is difficult because of her strict nature and difficulty adapting. But she will also take on all the household duties, and her husband can relax, knowing his children are in good hands.

Taurus, Pisces, and Scorpio make good matches. Aries is difficult, once things cool off after the initial honeymoon. When a Capricorn meets another Capricorn, they will be each other's first and last love. Sagittarius isn't a bad match, but they don't always pass the test of time. Aquarius and Capricorn are a difficult match, and rarely found together. Things are too dull with a Virgo, and while Leo can be exciting at first, things will fall apart when he begins showing off. Libra and Aquarius are both difficult partners for Capricorn, and she is rarely found with either of them.

AQUARIUS

A female Aquarius is very different from her male counterparts. She is calm and keeps a cool head, but she is also affectionate and open. She values loyalty above all else, and is unlikely to recover from any infidelity, though she will only divorce if this becomes a chronic trend, and she has truly been stabbed in the back. She is not interested in her partner's money, but rather, his professional success. She is unobtrusive and trusting, and will refrain from listening in on her partner's phone conversations or hacking into his email. With rare exceptions, Aquarian women make terrible housewives. But they are excellent partners in life – they are faithful, never boring, and will not reject a man, even in the most difficult circumstances. Most Aquarians are highly intuitive, and can easily tell the truth from a lie. They themselves only lie in extreme situations, which call for a "white lie" in order to avoid hurting someone's feelings.

Aquarius gets along well with Aries, Gemini, and Libra. She can also have a good relationship with a Sagittarius. Taurus often makes a successful match, though they are emotionally very different; the same goes for Virgo. Aquarius and Scorpio, Capricorn, or Cancer is a difficult match. Pisces can make a good partner as well, as both signs complement each other. Any relationship with a Leo will be tumultuous, but lasting, as Leo is selfish, and Aquarius will therefore have to be very forgiving.

PISCES

Pisces women are very adaptable, musically inclined, and erotic. They possess an innate earthly wisdom, and a good business sense. Pisces often reinvent themselves; they can be emotional, soft, and obstinate, as well as sentimental, at times. Their behavioral changes can be explained by frequent ups and downs. Pisces is charming, caring, and her outward malleability is very attractive to men. She is capable of loving selflessly, as long as the man has something to love. Even if he doesn't, she will try and take care of him until the very end. Pisces' greatest fear is poverty. They are intuitive, vulnerable, and always try to avoid conflict. They love to embellish the truth, and sometimes alcohol helps with this. Rarely, one finds extremely unbalanced, neurotic and dishonest Pisces, who are capable of turning their loved ones' lives into a living Hell!

Taurus, Capricorn, Cancer, and Scorpio make the best matches. She will be greatly attracted to a Virgo, but a lasting relationship is only likely if both partners are highly spiritual. Any union with a Libra is likely to be difficult and full of conflict. Pisces finds Gemini attractive, and they may have a very lively relationship – for a while. Occasionally, Pisces ends up with a Sagittarius, but she will have to fade into the background and entirely submit to him. If she ends up with an Aquarius, expect strong emotional outbursts, and a marriage that revolves around the need to raise their children.

Tatiana Borsch